VICTORY OVER SUFFERING

A Survivor's Story

CHRISTINA RYAN

Published by
New Creation Ministries
Lima, Ohio

VICTORY OVER SUFFERING

FIRST EDITION
Copyright © 1995 by
Christina Ryan

All rights reserved. No portion of this book may be reproduced or utilized in any form or by any means, electronic or mechanical including photocopying, without permission in writing from the publisher. Inquires should be addressed to: Rev. Christina Ryan, P.O. Box 715, Lima, Ohio 45802-0715.

Library of Congress Catalog Card Number: 95-92557

Scripture quotations are from the *King James Version of the Bible*, in the public domain.

"From *The New King James Version*. Copyright (c) 1979, 1980, 1982, Thomas Nelson Inc., Publishers."

Scripture quotations are from the *HOLY BIBLE, NEW INTERNATIONAL VERSION*. Copyright (c) 1973, 1978, 1984 International Bible Society. Used by permission of Zondervan Bible Publishers. All rights reserved.

Mike Lackey, Editor
JoAnne Koch, Consulting Editor
Ginni Guarnieri, Special Editor

Cover Art by Marge Brandt
Graphics by Michael Slone
Cover Photo - Four Seasons Photography, Lima, Ohio

ISBN 0-7880-0631-2   PRINTED IN U.S.A.

Dedicated to:

Grandma Celesta Giesken,
and to my son, Zachary
whose earthly love helped me to survive
before I met Jesus Christ,
The Savior of my Soul, and
the mender of my broken heart.

CONTENTS

FOREWORD

By Pastors Peter and Phyllis Doseck
Only Believe Ministries Christian Center
with Mike Lackey

When Christina Ryan first came to our church, her life was in ruins. She was emotionally broken. For years, she had been in and out of mental institutions. She was incapable of trusting other people, and she had a long way to go to learn to trust God.

What we didn't know then was that Christina was a classic example of a victim of physical and sexual abuse.

Traditionally, the Church has not done a good job of dealing with sexual abuse. We hate to acknowledge that any of us have been hurt or abused. Today, the Church is just learning to deal with all the abuse that has been under cover for years.

Many people, men as well as women, have been victims of sexual abuse. The repercussions of this abuse are all around us. Victims of abuse have a particularly hard time seeking and finding the love and healing God offers. They blame God for the tragedies that have befallen them. "God does not love me," they say. "If He did, He would not have allowed this to happen."

Christians inadvertently make it more difficult for abuse victims to come to God. Scripture is sometimes taken out of context to suggest that once a person gives his or her life to Christ, that person's past life should simply be forgotten. Perhaps the best example is Philippians 3:14...

"Forgetting those things which are behind, and reaching forth unto those things which are before."

It is true, of course, that Christians must be prepared to leave their past lives behind and reach forward toward new lives in Christ. But even when old sins and hurts are left behind, we still have to deal with their side effects—with feelings of shame or rejection, or with hatred for those who have assaulted us. We cannot simply sweep the past under the carpet; we must deal with it and give God a chance to heal us.

That is what this book is all about. For all her searching, Christina found no help until she turned to the Bible. She learned the lesson of Proverbs 4:22: The words of God <u>are life unto those that find them, and health to all their flesh</u>. God was not the cause of her pain; He is the solution.

God has worked a miracle of healing in Christina's life. But growth and healing haven't come quickly or easily. They have required commitment, prayer and diligence in applying the Word of God to her daily life.

Here, in <u>Victory over Suffering</u>, Christina shares the Scriptural keys to overcoming physical and sexual abuse. God has shown her the way. He waits to do the same for you.

INTRODUCTION

A young woman about twenty years old emotionally broke down at church. Her head lay on the back of the pew in front of her. Dark mid-length hair covered her face. Her thin body shook uncontrollably as she sobbed while the pastor began to preach.

The usher and I had both come from dysfunctional homes. Before our conversion to Christianity, we had attended the same Adult Children of Alcoholics' meetings. As we helped this girl outside, our eyes met. We knew what we were dealing with. This young woman was a victim, just as we had been. As I held her hand, I listened once again to the all too familiar story. I said, "That's it, God, I'll write the book."

The church has dramatically ignored the needs of this hurting population. The abused and dysfunctional come to our altars every week, crying out for God's help. We pray for God's peace in their lives, give them a hug and send them back to their pews, still troubled and afraid.

Jeremiah said, **"For they have healed the hurt of the daughter of my people slightly, saying, <u>Peace, Peace; when there is no peace.</u>" (Jeremiah 8:11)**

We must teach people to walk in the deliverance that Christ purchased at Calvary. In **Matthew 19:26**, Jesus said, **"With God, all things are possible."** Yet, you must be willing to go through the pain and be persistent in pursuit of wholeness.

There is no case too hopeless for Jesus Christ, our great physician. The medical people of the world labeled me incurable. Despite years of psychiatrists, psychologists, medications and institutionalization, there was one prognosis for my life. In 1986, the psychiatrist in charge of my case said I probably would die in a mental institution.

Then I met the most wonderful, amazing person, who is responsible for changing my life. His name is Jesus Christ. Jesus truly **"is the way, the truth, and the life." (John 14:6)** Through this book, I pray you will find the way to healing, utilizing the truth of God's word and His promise for abundant life.

9

We will look back upon events in my life and the lives of others just as we look back upon the wilderness experience of the children of Israel. God has taught me how to travel by the cloud by day and the pillar of fire at night.

With the Holy Spirit's guidance, it is my heart's desire to show the path to those of you still suffering. His word is truly the lamp for our feet and the light of our path. There is one question abuse victims ask more than any other: "If God really loves me, why did He allow all those bad things to happen to me?" Several years ago, God spoke to me in that still small voice and said, "Do not ask why. It makes you sick." He was referring to mental torment. By faith, I quit asking, and that is when the answer came.

One by one, God began to send men, women, and children along my path who were victims of abuse. Specifically, He sent those ravaged by sexual abuse and dysfunction.

Sexual abuse is difficult to trace, since many victims remain silent their entire lives. In Jan Frank's book, A Door of Hope,*1 she cites a 1985 Los Angeles Times survey which showed "that nearly one out of every four people in the United States have been molested as a child."*2

It takes only a few minutes for an abuser to molest a child, but a child can suffer a whole lifetime without God's healing. Sexual abuse is a selfish act of self-gratification that defies God's laws of natural affection. Adults are to nurture and protect children, not to exploit them.

I have shed many tears, wrestling with the anger and unforgiveness my abuse created. I will share the insight those tears have given me. In this book, we will explore the price you must pay to be whole.

My prayers are with you as you begin. If we do not meet on this earth, drop in my mansion in Heaven. It will be the 1800's brick with the antique wicker rocker on the porch. There will be lace curtains blowing in and out of the windowless sills. You see, Dear One, we will not need windows, or fences, or locks in Heaven. There will be no thief to break in and steal what belongs to us. Yet, on earth, Satan has stolen from so many.

I ask for God's anointing on the words that follow. May His

truth enable you to take back all the Wicked One has stolen from you, in Jesus Christ's precious name.

                              Love,
                                Christina

CHAPTER ONE

LOOKING BACK

I wandered lonely as a cloud
That floats on high o'er vales and hills,
When all at once I saw a crowd,
A host of golden daffodils;
Beside the lake, beneath the trees,
Fluttering and dancing in the breeze.

William Wordsworth, 1804

It was twenty years ago, but it is as if it were yesterday. It does not seem like my story, but rather the story of some poor victim of circumstance. This is, after all, what I was, a victim of circumstance. I can see myself sitting on that uncomfortable bench outside the nurses' station. Several nurses are enclosed in the glass cubicle rapidly writing reports. I was to find out that there were few "real" nurses.

In those days, state mental hospitals were not exactly desirable places to work. They were places the outcasts, the incurable, and the hopeless were housed. Yet, there I sat, a seventeen-year-old girl locked behind the doors of this institution. I didn't know how many hours it had been since Mom and Grandma dropped me off. But I knew they were not coming back.

I had come through admission and they had taken my small suitcase away. A female attendant made me remove even the clothes I was wearing. With a hose that seemed like it belonged on a fire truck, the "nurse" sprayed me like an animal. It was a precaution to make sure body mites were not brought into the hospital. She sprayed white powder over my entire body. Then, the nurse gave me a matronly blue dress that looked like it had been borrowed from the local prison. She escorted me to the ward that was to be my home in the months to come.

For hours, I sat on that bench, willing my mom and my grandma back. I remember desperately trying to visualize the scene that gave me peace back then. It was a field of daffodils swaying gently in the breeze. Many times, when things became chaotic, I retreated into my mind and pictured my precious daffodils. But this day, my daffodils gave me no joy. I was trying to understand why I was here. How had I come to this?

I had spent the last two or three months on the psychiatric ward of a local hospital. The hospital looked like a luxury hotel in comparison to this decaying institution. My insurance must have been running out at the private hospital, so I was sent home. I was home less than a week when I dug at my wrist with a razor blade. I did not do this in an attempt to end my life. I did it because of anger and hurt. Satan had made sure I overheard a phone conversation between my mother and my uncle, a non-Christian psychiatrist in Toledo, Ohio. They were planning to institutionalize me, as they feared I had not "gotten well" at the hospital. Looking back, my mother must have been terrified that if left to my own devices, I would try to end my life.

She had almost lost me two years earlier, when I was fifteen. I overdosed on tranquilizers the family doctor had given me for my "nerves." I had taken the entire prescription, then gone to bed to die. When she couldn't wake me, Mom realized what I had done. She called an ambulance, but because of the quantity of pills I had swallowed, I hovered between life and death in the hospital's intensive care unit.

At one point, I heard someone say I was dying, but I knew I was going to live. Even in my semi-conscious state, I heard a voice inside me clearly say, "You're such a loser, you can't even kill yourself."

For several years, I do not remember talking with my mother. But inside, my being cried out for her to help me. I was so outraged that she could not see my pain. Now, I know sadly that people cannot read other people's minds, even the minds of their own children.

Why would a young teenager spend her days plotting her own destruction? That was the question in the heart of my bewildered family and confused friends.

More importantly, where was God in the midst of this tragedy? When I was 7, I told God that I would serve Him and do what He wanted. I was a devout Catholic child, taught to revere God. I believed God was good, and that He would always be there for me. My prayer to serve Him was the fervent prayer of a determined little girl with a pure heart for her God.

But that pure heart was broken by years of living in an alcoholic home. One devastating night, every hope within me was shattered. It was the night the satanic spirit of perversion targeted me for sexual abuse. There was something that broke within me as I defended my little body from my abuser's advances.

I remember that I wore pajamas of pink and white striped cotton hemmed with lace. Before that night, I thought they were beautiful. Afterwards, I was to find nothing beautiful for years.

As a child, I watched my adult abuser struggle to overcome the spirit that drove him. He would wrestle with it, conquer it, then it would reappear.

What had I done to make this trusted relative feel this way? I must be terribly bad or this would never have happened. Surely it was my fault. I was so ashamed of the thing in me that caused it, I knew I must be punished.

That is exactly what I did. I punished myself for years. I became self-destructive. I allowed myself little laughter as other children knew. I was bad and I must be destroyed. It is not logical, but it happened.

Healthy children have an innate ability to tell right from wrong. They also possess a mechanism, which I once heard a counselor describe as the "ah-oh" feeling. Children are acutely aware of dangerous situations and devious people with wrong intentions.

Early victimization will confuse a child's ability to differentiate between right and wrong, and recognize who is trustworthy or not. Sexual abuse also can birth a host of spirits that gradually destroy a victim's life. Abused children are overwhelmed by rage. Their fragile idealism is shattered by the unfairness of life creating a severe imbalance inside of them. They become angry, rebellious, and self-destructive.

When the victimization is perpetrated by a trusted relative or friend, the child's ability to trust or perceive basic values is also destroyed. The child retreats into his or her own isolated reality: a reality full of pain, shame and suffering. Often, children assume the guilt that belongs to the victimizer, and they bottle their feelings: "If I wasn't bad, this wouldn't have happened to me."

Children's bodies are no different than adult bodies. When a child is molested, or a man or woman is raped, the body often enjoys the physical sensation. Therefore, they come to falsely believe, "If I am not guilty, how could my body respond to the unwanted advance?" The body is a machine. It is no different than a typewriter. If I punch a key, a certain response is elicited.

Sexual abuse is not necessarily rape. In my definition, it **is any unsolicited and inappropriate sexual advance that violates the privacy and rights of another human being.**

Physical abuse does not always culminate in a black eye or a broken jaw, either. Often, the most confused victims of abuse are those who have been verbally battered. They have been told for so many years that they are stupid, bad and ugly that they become defeated people with broken spirits. Yet, because they have no tangible scars, they discount the severity of their abuse.

Frequently, when children have been hurt, they begin to hurt themselves. By age nine, I remember hitting myself in the face very hard and scratching my arms with my fingernails until my little arms would bleed.

Body mutilation is often a sign of sexual abuse. Please take your Bible and read the fifth chapter of Mark about the demoniac at the tombs in the country of Gadarenes, who was crying and cutting himself day and night.

> **"When they arrived at the other side of the lake a demon-possessed man ran out from a graveyard, just as Jesus was climbing from the boat. This man lived among the gravestones, and had such strength that whenever he was put into handcuffs and shackles — as often as he was — he snapped the handcuffs from his wrists and smashed the shackles and walked away. No one was strong enough to control him. All day long and through the night he would wander among the tombs and in the wild hills, screaming and cutting himself with sharp pieces of stone."**
> **(Mark 5:1-5 NKJ)**

By age 17, there was a rage inside of me that could not be contained. Mom had seen evidence of razor cuts on my arms before. I was controlled by rage. That rage has a name, I found out later. It was the unclean spirit that possessed the demonic man at the tombs.

I don't remember how I felt about God. I only remember feeling that He was very far away. I did not know that in hundreds of different ways, God had said in the Bible that He would never forsake me. I had never seen His word. I had been taught "religion," but I had not seen the Bible. I had never heard of a personal relationship with Jesus, nor did I know that Satan was real. To me, he was some kind of mythical creature detached from reality. I was ignorant of the Devil's devices. I didn't know that all the hurt and evil in my life had been the result of a direct attack by Satan to destroy me.

So that is how it all began. By the age of 17, a senior in high school, I was diagnosed as "mentally ill." I did not get a part in the school play or invitations to senior parties. I lived in a state institution full of every type of evil spirit Satan employs.

My first day there, I was taken to the infirmary for a physical examination. We stood in long lines much like those photographed in German prison camps of World War II. I saw a young woman waiting to see the "doctor." I use quotation marks, as I have never seen a poorer excuse for a doctor than that brash, dirty man. He swore loudly and wasted no time being gentle. The young woman had been bitten on the face and her nose was hanging unattached where the teeth marks were.

When I saw her, any glimmer of hope evaporated. I knew I would not survive this place. I retreated into myself and quit eating, so that I would die sooner.

Day after day, I waited for someone from my family to come. I was seventy-five miles from home, and it felt as if they were a continent away. Even though my home was full of dysfunctional pain, it was familiar.

Day after day, no one came. I counted, and by day eleven, I had not seen any family member, or doctor, unless you want to call the man in the infirmary a doctor. During those eleven days, I had not had a shower or washed my long hair. I wore the same matronly blue dress that they had put on me in admitting. It had not been washed, either.

I don't know how Jesus felt when He was dying on the cross, but I know that He knows how I felt then. Even though I did not know Him, I can look back and see that He did not allow Satan to try me beyond what I could bear. It was on the eleventh day, when I could no longer go on, that doors began to open.

I was ushered in to see a graying psychiatrist. He appeared to have compassion for me. He moved me from the large ward room that I shared with four other extremely disturbed women.

There were only two private rooms on that floor, and I was given the tiny pink room that would become my haven in the months to come. Although the windows were heavily barred with wrought iron and wire, I could see outside.

I began to eat my meals, my belongings were returned, and I was allowed to shower. Even though I had been forsaken by every human being I depended on, I felt a reassuring presence for a short time, just when I could no longer stand. Now, I know God's Holy Spirit was making the way for me, when I was too confused to find the path.

A few years ago, when I was looking back on the experiences of youth, and trying desperately not to ask "why?", God showed me a wonderful Scripture. **Psalm 27:10** says, **"When my father and mother forsake me, then the Lord will take me up."** God warns us in the books of Psalms and Micah that we should put our trust in Him, not in a man or woman. When we do, He is able to lift us up past the circumstance. Today, I am no longer a victim of circumstance. Through God, I am victorious in the midst of circumstance.

I have shared a few of the tragic moments of my life, not to dwell on the things of the past, but so that you could understand that I understand suffering. One excuse I used for years was that no one had it as bad as I did, or that no one understood my pain. There are many victims of abuse, and many people who are products of dysfunction. We must be willing to reach out to each other for healing.

Several years ago, I became friendly with a Catholic nun who taught a Bible study. We shared a love for antique furniture and thrift stores, and enjoyed talking with one another. One day, I realized she was not well. She explained she would need an operation soon, and I could see that she was already afflicted with a type of palsy.

"Sister," I said, "I'm so sorry that you are suffering so much."

She smiled and said quite matter-of-factly, "Well, I've never met anyone that was worth very much that hasn't gone through a lot of adversity."

That's the key. We have to "go through" adversity, not get stuck in it.

In Revelations, we are told that **"They overcame him (the devil) by the blood of the Lamb, the word of their testimony, and that they feared not their lives to death." (Rev 12:11)** This book is the word of my testimony.

There is a big part of me that would like to deny my roots. I'm sorry that some things in this book might cause hurt. For some members of my family, speaking truthfully of the past is a form of treason. But God can't help us unless we are completely honest with Him. You must stop right now and make a decision to be honest with your heavenly Father.

In a dysfunctional home, a great deal of energy is focused on presenting an appearance of normality. Children learn at a tender age to lie in order to protect the unhealthy behaviors of their parents. If Dad has a hangover, and is unable to speak on the phone, the child will be told to tell callers, "Daddy has the flu." If Dad gives Mom a black eye, the child is included in the "Mommy fell down" lie.

Initially, these lies are a type of glue to create a cohesive environment out of chaos. Unfortunately, as children grow, they become unable to distinguish between the truth and the lie. As Isaiah the prophet said, they begin to **"call evil good, and good evil." (Isaiah 5:20)** This trait will carry over into their relationships with others as they mature. It will prevent children of dysfunction from enjoying healthy communication which is the basis for all relationships.

Dysfunction is too civilized a word to express the "Hell on earth" millions of adults and children experience each day. In one area or another, most of us have experienced some degree of dysfunction. For decades Webster's Dictionary has defined dysfunction as impaired or abnormal functioning. I define **dysfunction as a direct Satanic attack upon the family unit, resulting in emotionally fragmented people, generation after generation.**

Being products of dysfunction makes us prime targets for a life of victimization. For our sakes, and the sakes of our children, we must allow Christ to set us free. In **Luke 4:18**, Jesus said, **"The spirit of the Lord is upon me, because He hath anointed me to preach the gospel to the poor; He hath sent me to heal the**

brokenhearted, to preach deliverance to the captives and recovering of sight to the blind."

We have been poor in spirit, brokenhearted and bound for long enough. He has come to heal not only our physical, but our spiritual blindness. For too many years, we have not seen who we are in Christ, or the plan He has for each one of our lives. My prayer for you today is that your eyes will be opened to all that He desires to do for you, in Jesus' name.

CHAPTER TWO

ABUSED AND ABUSER

PSALM 37

Do not fret because of evil men
  or be envious of those who do wrong;
For like the grass they will soon wither,
  like green plants they will soon die away.

Trust in the Lord and do good;
  dwell in the land and enjoy safe pasture.
Delight yourself in the Lord
  and He will give you the desires of your heart.

Commit your way to the Lord;
  trust in Him and He will do this:
He will make your righteousness shine
      like the dawn
the justice of your cause like the noonday sun.

(New International Version)

David is a 39-year-old man who appears to have it all together. For twenty years, he has had the same job in a factory that provides his family with an excellent lifestyle. He is kind to his children, good to his second wife. He even takes care of his aging mother, who lives nearby.

Despite the outward appearance of tranquilty, a host of tormenting spirits buffet David daily. Outwardly, he is a confident man; inwardly, he is a little boy with a broken heart.

Several years ago, I sat on David's porch as the cool summer breeze gently surrounded us. He married my friend, who has a son close to my son's age. As David and I chatted, the boys asked to go down the street to visit a neighbor.

When they asked permission, I said, "I don't know."

When led by the Holy Spirit, I am open with the hurts of my life. I said, "I know I seem overly protective to people, but I was sexually abused as a child. I don't trust people I don't know with my son."

Immediately, David looked up and said, "I was sexually abused as a child, too. My mother molested me when I was 10."

In that one sentence, I heard the heartbreak that had changed that dear man's life. In the next hour came the questions I have come to know so well.

"How could anything so disgusting, feel (physically) good?"

"How can you learn to trust others, especially God?"

One by one we discussed the questions that are common to victims.

I explained that the body is a machine, and when touched in certain places, it responds. I told David it was sad, but parents and those in authority can treat children any way they choose. I told him he could throw his own son against a wall in anger and God probably wouldn't stop it. I explained it would sadden God greatly, but children are at the mercy of those who care for them.

When I left David's house that night, something in my vision had been rearranged. Over the years, I had come to know many homosexual men. Always, it was the same story when we would communicate on an intimate level. The homosexual had been sexually abused in some way as a child, or had had no male figure in his life whatsoever.

I had known lesbian women who had been abused as children, too. An 18-year-old girl who was fighting a lesbian spirit stayed with us for a short time. This young woman had been sexually abused by her father as a child. Later, unable to cope with the victimization, she had been hospitalized. She was raped by one of the workers at the psychiatric hospital. She was so terrified of men, that she began to seek relationships with women.

In a recent article in Today's Christian Woman, mother Kathleen Bremner discussed her adult daughter's lesbianism. Author Candace Walters narrated Mrs. Bremner's struggle to accept her daughter's overt defiance of God's law.

Ms. Walters quotes Mrs. Bremner saying, "One day, when I was at my lowest and the pain seemed unbearable, I met with Barbara Johnson, author of Where Does a Mother Go to Resign? (Bethany House). Her book chronicles her struggle to cope with her son's homosexuality. Barbara explained homosexuality is a condition with such deep and diverse causes that no mother should hold herself responsible for 'making another person gay.' God knows I made plenty of mistakes in parenting--and I'm sure, as with many lesbians, Susan's sexual abuse was a contributing factor. But homosexual behavior is first and foremost an individual's choice."[1]

Prior to my friendship with several homosexual men, I had assumed that victims of sexual abuse were always female. This ill-founded theory was not based on information, rather on circumstantial evidence. But God soon changed my theory. He showed me that heterosexual men had been victimized as boys, too. Not only were they victims, but women were sometimes the victimizers.

In the April 1993 Redbook magazine, Glenna Whitley drew a vivid portrait of the adolescent boy as a victim. "Just 10 years ago, female child molesters were considered rare," Ms. Whitley wrote in "The Seduction of Donnie Porter."

"Experts now know better: Approximately 24 percent of all male victims and 13 percent of female victims of child sexual abuse are molested by women acting alone or with a male partner."[2] Whitley further states that there are three types of female sex offenders, according to Jane Matthews, a St. Paul psychologist who treats female abusers. The 1) <u>male-coerced</u> offender who acts with a man; 2) the <u>intergenerational</u>, who repeats history of family victimization; and 3) the <u>teacher/lover</u> category.

Matthews says the woman in the <u>teacher/lover</u> category is not aware of her wrongdoing. "She believes she's giving the boy a tremendous gift by teaching him about sex. All too often society agrees. While few people would approve of an adult man seducing a young girl, the idea of a woman initiating a boy into manhood is widely accepted."*3

"The Secuction of Donnie Porter" is the true story of a 36-year-old Cub Scout den mother enticing a 12-year-old boy. Donnie Porter's story is an example of this teacher/lover category. Author Glenna Whitley portrays the woman as a trusted family friend who seduces the boy. This affair was to last almost two years. Today, at 15, Donnie Porter is in therapy. His abuser is serving a prison sentence, but continues to assert her innocence, according to the <u>Redbook</u> article.*4

Donnie Porter's story gave me insight into the tragic tale of another young man who attended my church. For years I watched Brian (not his real name) struggle to maintain a lifestyle of holiness. For months he would be faithful, then he would meet a young woman and fall into sin. He would be broken-hearted, repent, and sever the ungodly relationship. Then, in a short time, he would find himself trapped once again by sexual sin. Brian genuinely desired to serve God. He even felt he was called to the ministry. Yet, his sexual desire frustrated him and made him think it was too big even for God.

Most Christians would condemn Brian for his sin, never seeing the force that motivated the sin. He, too, had been a victim of sexual abuse. Brian was 12 years old when his cousin, a young married woman, seduced him. She became angry when Brian, only a boy, could not physically satisfy her. He spent his entire life following that incident trying to prove his malehood by being sexually proficient.

Brian believed this incident with his cousin would never have occurred if his father had not died. Brian's dad died when he was 10. His mother became immersed in the responsibility of being the sole breadwinner. Brian was left alone and vulnerable to the plan that Satan had devised.

Until we talked, Brian had not realized he had been sexually abused. Because of the double standard we mentioned earlier, Brian felt his cousin had merely indoctrinated him into the realm of sexuality. In reality, Satan had used this woman to destroy the innocence of childhood for Brian. Brian suggested I use his story to help other men who have been victims, too.

For far too long we have looked at males as abusers and at females as victims. God wants us to be able to help our suffering brothers who have been victims, too. After all, in **Galatians 3:28**, we are told, that **"There is neither Jew nor Greek, there is neither bond nor free, there is neither male nor female: for ye are all one in Christ Jesus."**

One of Satan's greatest lies is that boys are not hurt by early sexual victimization. In Genesis 39 we find the story of Joseph and Potipahr's wife. Joseph was a young man sold into slavery by his jealous brothers. He was taken to Egypt, where he found favor with the captain of the guard, Potiphar.

Potiphar made Joseph overseer over his house, giving Joseph responsibility for all he owned. Then Potiphar's wife began making sexual advances to Joseph, which he rejected. Potiphar's wife became so angry at Joseph that one day she grabbed him by the coat and demanded sex. He fled the house, with the lustful woman still clutching his coat. She then fabricated a story that Joseph had tried to rape her, using his coat as evidence. The innocent young man was cast into prison, where he remained for several years, until he gained his freedom by interpreting the Pharaoh's dream.

We are not told how old Joseph was when this incident happened. We know Joseph was still in his father's house, an unmarried youth, when he was sold into slavery.

When Potiphar's wife tried to force him into a sexual relationship, Joseph showed great strength and purity of heart in refusing her advances and suffering imprisonment. Most males who have been abused were too young and too impressionable to run from their abusers. Yet they, like Joseph, have lived for years in the prison abuse creates.

Male victims are no different from female victims. Their hearts are broken and their inner core of trust is destroyed. Whether the victimization occurs at 2 or 12, the result is the same: a confused and hurting child.

However, the age of the abuser is significant. Often, abused children will abuse others. We will address children as abusers in the chapter on "Forgiveness."

Another example of sexual abuse occurs in Scripture in the 13th chapter of 2 Samuel. Here we are introduced to a young girl named Tamar, King David's daughter and Absalom's sister. David also has another son, Amnon, who is Tamar and Absalom's brother.

Amnon began to desire Tamar. **"Amnon was so vexed, that he fell sick for his sister Tamar; for she was a virgin; and Amnon thought it hard for him to do any thing to her." (2 Samuel 13:2)** But Amnon became overcome with his lust and along with another friend, Jonadab, he plotted the rape of Tamar.

Amnon pretended to be ill and asked his father David to send Tamar to prepare food for him in his chamber. The unsuspecting Tamar found herself alone in her brother's bedroom, and Amnon asked his sister to, **"Come and lie with me."** (**2 Samuel 13:11**) The word **"lie"** in this Scripture is from the Hebrew word shakab, which literally means a lying down for the sexual act.*5

Tamar pleaded with Amnon, asking him not to force her into this incestuous act. Moses already had authored the Book of Leviticus, which forbade sexual intercourse between a brother and a sister. (Leviticus, 18:9-11) But Amnon gave in to his desire and, **"being stronger than she, forced her, and lay with her." (2 Samuel 13:14)**

The next Scripture in this sad tale is very interesting. It says, **"Then Amnon hated her exceedingly; so that the hatred where- with he hated her was greater than the love wherewith he had loved her." (2 Samuel 13:15)** As soon as Amnon had fulfilled his lustful desire upon his sister, he no longer loved her. He literally despised her and cast her from his presence.

Tamar, brokenhearted, went to her brother Absalom's house. Absalom realized what had happened and told her to **"hold now thy peace, my sister: he is thy brother; regard not this thing.**

So Tamar remained desolate in her brother Absalom's house. But when King David heard of all these things, he was very wroth. And Absalom spake unto his brother Amnon neither good nor bad: for Absalom hated Amnon, because he had forced his sister Tamar." (2 Samuel 13:20-22)   In this biblical account we find Tamar the victim, who is devastated, yet told by her brother Absalom to remain quiet rather than destroy the reputation of the household. We find King David, a strong man of God, a man of battles, who literally does nothing to confront this episode.

We see the result of the sins of the fathers being visited upon the children as stated in Exodus 34:7. David himself had been unable to contain his sexual desire for Bathsheba, another man's wife. David had Bathsheba's husband killed in order to be free to marry her.

David's iniquities or weaknesses are apparent in the life of his son, Amnon. Because long ago David failed this same moral test, he is not able to confront this sin with Amnon.

In the same way, what happens often today happened thousands of years ago to Tamar. She was silenced, forced to hold her pain in and maintain a desolate lifestyle. Amnon was not confronted with the sin he had committed. Therefore, he had no opportunity to endure the consequences of that sin, which could have offered him an eventual door to repentance, if he could be convinced of his wrongdoing. Absalom seethed with hatred for Amnon and eventually killed him.

Because of the sexual sin of Amnon, his family was destroyed, and eventually he lost his own life as the price for his sin. Since, according to our <u>Redbook</u> survey, the largest percentage of abusers are male,*6 we will use Amnon as a study in how we should treat the abuser. It is important that since Tamar and Amnon were brother and sister, there must have been a relationship based on love before this rape occurred.

Let's return to **2 Samuel 13:15, "Then Amnon hated her exceedingly; so that the hatred wherewith he hated her was greater than the love wherewith he had loved her."** This statement proves there was an underlying relationship of love prior to Tamar's rape. After Amnon raped her, he wanted her removed from his presence, but she begged him not to treat her in such a fashion. Love is a fragile emotion, but when it is based on God's Word it endures even violation.

Amnon could not stand the sight of Tamar because he could not stand what he had done to her. His own guilt caused him to look at her with disgust. Even though Tamar was devastated, she grieved not only for the loss of her virginity, but for the loss of relationship with a brother who had once been her friend, a brother who had seen an ungodly example by his father in terms of sexual relationship.

This is all hypothetical, as we will never truly know how Tamar felt. Yet those of us who have been victimized by someone we love will tell you, the love does not stop. Yes, without God's intervention, it will appear to be hatred. You must realize that when love truly dies, it does not become hatred, it becomes detached and indifferent. Hatred is a sign that there is still love as the basis of the emotion. Human love can survive brutal abuse. So surely, God's love is greater than any crime ever committed.

For a few moments we will travel back thousands of years. We find Tamar weeping unconsolably in the house of Absalom. It has been months since Amnon raped her and she feels as if there are to be no more tomorrows for her. Her hope was destroyed in that instant. Later, as Absalom and David silenced her, she retreated into herself, weeping for all that was lost.

But this day is different. Absalom is not pacing the halls looking at her with that pathetic expression that says, "You'll never be the same." On this day, the blood of her warrior father David courses through her veins. She will take action. She once thought of killing Amnon, but Absalom's constant anger and continued promise of vengeance have helped her see how unsatisfactory hurting Amnon would be.

She remembers Amnon when they were tiny children. She remembers playing in the palace pool, fighting for toys, and dunking one another as their nursemaids looked on in amusement. She thinks, too, of the horses David bought for them. The groom said she was a girl and could not learn to ride, but Amnon threatened him with the voice of a prince, and she too had riding lessons.

They had been left alone so much by their royal parents. Their father had too many wives and too much business with the kingdom. He had no time for raising children, so they had raised each other. They had been friends, companions, and family.

But then Tamar had begun to develop physically, and Amnon started to look at her differently. She had wondered a million times why she had not seen it in his eyes, the lust that had destroyed their innocent relationship. Well, it was over now. She could not spend the rest of her life crying. She dried her eyes and went to her chamber. Her handmaiden hovered at her side. All the servants in the palace knew what had happened to her. But no one spoke of it.

This day, however, she did not want her handmaiden to attend her. She wanted to be alone. She wanted to do what she knew she must do. She had prayed to the God of Abraham, Issac, and Jacob. She had prayed to the God who had so often forgiven her father's transgressions and had continued to love and use the warrior king. God had answered her and told her she must let go of her hurt. She could not destroy any more of her life by weeping day after day. She must trust her heavenly Father as she never had, even though her earthly father had failed her and all those around her had failed her.

So Tamar sat down at the small ornate mahogany desk in her chamber. She opened the top drawer with her key and pulled out a vial of precious ink her father had brought her from India. Then she took the parchment that she saved for those special to her. She picked up the quill pen that had a golden writing point and a long plumed feather. She dipped the pen's gold tip into the ink and began to write:

Dearest Amnon,

With God's help, I will share my heart with you, my brother. Despite what has happened between us, you are still my brother. I have tried hating you and denying our kinship, but our father's blood connects us. Not only our earthly father, but our heavenly Father commands that we trust in Him, and allow Him to be the avenger of our wrongs.

I began to think of you as my enemy, by brother. When our father, David, wrote the Book of Psalms, he spoke of enemies who had once been friends. Father did not seek to destroy them, rather he praised God that God would deliver him from their evil works. I have prayed that God would deliver me from the evil work that has been done to me.

After months of praying for you, I began to see that it was not you that was my enemy. After all you, too, have been a victim of the wicked one. I know you once loved me greatly. I know that my words brought comfort to you on many occasions. Now there is no more communication between us. There is a gulf of silence that could span a lifetime if we do not acknowledge what has happened.

Amnon, you took from me what no man had the right to take. You have done a wicked thing, but God is able to forgive you. I know God is able to forgive you, because I have forgiven you through Him. You see, Amnon, as I wept day after day, and became bitter for what you had done to me, I perceived a change in my countenance. It was gradual at first, then it became more pronounced. The lines around my mouth formed a cynical sneer, and the sparkle in my hazel eyes was replaced by the vacant look of a muddy field. But it was inside that was the worst. The constant gnawing pain of anger and unforgiveness churned like a demonic force day and night.

I have seen that force completely overtake Absalom these last months. He rages, and paces, and threatens to kill you at every opportunity. I have begged him to let go of this hatred, as it is of no benefit to any of us. Seeing him so consumed made me realize that I do not want to spend my remaining days as an unforgiving lunatic. For truly if I do not forgive you, Amnon, I shall go mad.

The wicked one has taken enough from me. I shall let him have no more. He will no longer control my days and nights. I have made a decision to forgive you so that I can be free to go on with my life. This decision will not reverse what has happened, however. I will not come to you alone ever again, unless God shows me there is a need for that. I will not jeopardize myself or my future children by the wicked spirit that you have allowed to overtake your life.

I will always pray for you, and believe God can convict you of this wrong you've done. Not so you will see my hurt, but so you can be freed of the sin that is yours. I do love you, Amnon, that has not changed.

Tamar

CHAPTER THREE

FEAR

THAT MEN SHOULD FEAR

Cowards die many times before death;
The valiant never taste of death but once.
Of all the wonders that I yet have heard,
It seems to me most strange that men should fear,
Seeing that death, a necessary end,
Will come when it will come.

William Shakespeare
from Julius Caesar

Until Christ set me free, I was immobilized by fear so terrifying it controlled my every moment. Let me backtrack to 1986. I find myself once more committed to a psychiatric facility. Although I have not been hospitalized for almost ten years, I have become sick again. It is probably the twelfth time I have been hospitalized and that gnawing fear is again my tormenting companion.

In 1986, I did not know that there is a Scripture that says, **"There is no fear in love, but perfect love casteth out fear." (I John 4:18)** You must not merely know about Jesus, as I did then. You must be acquainted with Him as Lord and Savior of your life.

What I knew about Him was very vague. Many bad things had happened in my life. Satan had deceived me into believing that God intensely disliked me or was totally indifferent to my well-being. Either way, I figured it was best to stay out of His path. Sometimes, I felt angry and hurt and screamed at Him that all-consuming question that destroys faith: "Why?"

By this point in my life, I was more afraid of living than of dying. Years earlier, I tried suicide several times and had been in the intensive care unit more than once. I felt I was such a failure that I could not even kill myself. What I did not know was that God had a plan for me, a wonderful plan to make me whole and well.

I did not really want to die. I had been given a precious little boy I adored. But I became convinced through Satan's lies that I could be no earthly good to my son. That is when God stepped in. He sent a pastor to the psychiatric ward to visit me. He told me about Jesus. He told me, too, that God was going to heal all the abuse I had been through. He said God was going to use me to minister to others.

I thought that pastor needed psychiatric help. I could not imagine how I could ever help others when I was incapable of taking care of even my own basic needs. Thank God that He sees our potential, not just our condition or circumstances. Pastor Dave Thompson had seen me through God's eyes; he saw what God was about to do with me. He asked another young man from the church to visit me at the hospital. That young man, who is today a pastor himself, came to my hospital room almost daily for the next several months. Once, perceiving that I was unable to accept that he was motivated purely by God's love, he brought his beautiful wife to reassure me they just wanted to see me well. Most abuse victims are very distrustful of the motives of others. (See chapter on trust.)

This young man, Gary Myers, would sit with me and just listen. When I would cry as I was sharing, I would see the pain reflected in his eyes. The Bible says we are to **"Rejoice with them that do rejoice and weep with them that weep." (Romans 12:15)**

Some of the things I said to that young preacher were not pleasant for him to hear. A man or woman of righteousness hates unrighteousness. However, we have to be willing to listen to others share their hurts so that God can begin to heal them. When we hear the terrible violations that people have endured, we must hold their hands, dry their tears, and validate that what they went through was horrendous. We must reassure them that God was sickened at the violation too, then we must point them to God's word.

This is exactly what Pastor Gary did. At the time, my depression was so severe I had become unable to read. The words in the Bible all blurred together. When I viewed my surroundings, it was as though I was looking through a black and white television. It seemed as if those who spoke to me were in a tunnel far away. The side effects of medication given for depression often cause visual problems, but I did not know that then.

All I knew was I could not read and was ashamed that I was so ill. I was a thirty-two year old corporate representative with a college degree. I had fought valiantly the last ten years to overcome the stigma of mental illness that had followed me through my late teens.

One day in my frustration, I told Pastor Gary that I could not read the Bible because I could not see the words. I began to cry. He seemed extremely pensive for a moment. Then he jumped up and began to write in very large letters on a small blackboard in the hospital room.

"Can you see this?" he asked.

Although Gary Myers was young, he was very wise concerning the devil's devices. He understood that we were fighting a spritual battle, and that our weapons are all outlined in Ephesians:

"Finally, my brethren, be strong in the Lord and in the power of His might. Put on the whole armor of God, that you may be able to stand against the wiles of the devil. For we do not wrestle against flesh and blood, but against principalities, against powers, against the rulers of the darkness of this age, against spiritual hosts of wickedness in the heavenly places. Therefore take up the whole armor of God, that you may be able to withstand in the evil day, and having done all, to stand. Stand therefore, having girded your waist with truth, having put on the breastplate of righteousness, and having shod your feet with the preparation of the gospel of peace; above all, taking the shield of faith with which you will be able to quench all the fiery darts of the wicked one. And take the helmet of salvation, and the sword of the Spirit, which is the word of God: praying always with all prayer and supplication in the Spirit, being watchful to this end with all perseverance and supplication for all saints." (Ephesians 6:10-18 NKJ) Please take several minutes to study these Scriptures now, to understand what I am about to share.

In Corinthians, the Apostle Paul tells us, **"Our weapons are not carnal, but mighty through God to the pulling down of strongholds." (2 Corinthians 10:4)** The weapons Paul referred to are the Word, prayer, fasting, and the blood and name of Christ. We are not in a battle with people, rather we are fighting Satan himself: **"For we wrestle (fight) not against flesh and blood, but against principalities and powers, against the rulers of the darkness of this world." (Ephesians 6:12)** Satan's legion of demons who try to destroy us are fear, depression, unfounded guilt, self-loathing, suicide, and a host of others.

Brother Myers would write only one Scripture a day on the small blackboard, large enough so that I could read it. (Sometimes, well-meaning Christians confuse people who are hurting with too many Scriptures and too little love.) I would study, meditate, and try to memorize each Scripture. One of the first he taught me was **2 Timothy 1:7**: **"For God has not given us a spirit of fear, but of power, of love, and of a sound mind."** I did not realize that simple Scripture would become of integral importance as I fought my way to freedom through God's word.

When I gave my heart to Jesus Christ and asked Him to be my Lord and Savior, He placed a helmet of salvation upon my head. That helmet, accompanied by the shield of faith, is our literal protection against the fiery darts of torment that Satan shoots at our minds. Satan attacks us with vicious, ungodly thoughts that must be rebuked and cast out in Jesus' name, providing we are not activating those thoughts through our own sin.

In addition, we must utilize the sword of the spirit, which is the word of God, to begin to walk a victorious Christian life.

Abuse victims do not only not live in victory, but often the bondage of fear leads them into a desperate lifestyle. For years, I was terrified of being by myself. If I was alone at night, I would drag large pieces of furniture in front of the door, trying to block the entry of an unknown predator. I would walk the floor, listening for signs of a break-in. At times I would think I heard footsteps, and I would be enveloped by a fear so real I would almost collapse. If I dozed off without some type of medication, I would often awaken in the middle of the night drenched in cold sweat, my heart beating so wildly I thought I was having some kind of attack.

When I became a Christian, it was no coincidence that one of the first Scriptures Pastor Gary taught me was **2 Timothy 1:7**. When the devil would wake me in the middle of the night to torment me, I would repeat over and over, **"God has not given me a spirit of fear, but of power, of love, and of a sound mind."** I would have to repeat this verse dozens of times before the peace of God would once again envelop me.

Sometimes, when I had fought the devil of fear all night, I would be so exhausted in the morning, I could barely function. In **Isaiah 54:17**, God tells us, **"No weapon formed against us shall prosper."** He also says in the fourteenth verse of the same chapter, **"In righteousness thou shall be established: thou shall be far from oppression; for thou shall not fear: and from terror; for it shall not come near thee."**

In Isaiah 54, the Lord also tells us He is our husband and that His kindness and covenant of peace shall not depart from us. I began to pray for a revelation of God's protective hand in my life. I saw that the Word said He would protect me. I believed it in my heart, but doubt was still lodged in my mind. In God's mercy, He saw that I did not want to be bound by the fear that was destroying my life.

Fear can not only cause sleepless nights. Often it immobilizes our ability to fulfill the goals and visions that God gives us. I was more blessed than most victims of fear, because my fear seemed to operate solely during the midnight hours. When the sun was out, I was bold in Christ to do whatever He had called me to. After the sun went down, however, I was a cowering mess.

A young man named William occasionally stopped in at my thrift/antique store and helped me move furniture. This young man saw me as a bold warrior in Christ. The day I asked for his prayers to combat the spirit of fear in my life, he was perplexed. I told him I had been sexually abused as a child, and I had fought fear my whole life. I told him, too, that I no longer wanted to be bound by the pride that pretended that everything was all right when it was not. I shared that I had to drag furniture to barracade my door and that I rarely slept, listening for footsteps on the stairs.

What I did not share with him was that I spent time with people who were not worthy of my time. Friends and family members belittled me, but I would spend hours with them to avoid being alone. I am so saddened when I see Christians allowing others to abuse them just so they won't be alone. This is how Satan sets us up to be repeatedly victimized. Then comes more shame, more fear, and a never-ending cycle.

My friend William was quite a prayer warrior, and also a trust-worthy confidant. He prayed and commanded the spirit of fear to go, but then I know he continued to pray. He did not know how to teach me to walk free of fear, as he had never been controlled by it, but he prayed God would show me.

As we serve a faithful God, who meets us at our point of need, the Holy Spirit had my pastor begin a series of teachings on fear at this time. Pastor Peter Doseck said something that I wrote down one night. "Fear has a root, and torment is always his brother." He went on to say, "We must remember we are in all these things more than conquerors through Him that loved us."*1

I realized I had to get to the root. I realized too that Christ had said I was more than a conqueror in any situation. I had a revelation that we must guard our hearts and minds through Jesus. As Apostle Paul told the Philippians, **"We must think only on those things true, just, pure, lovely, virtuous and full of good report." (Philippians 4:8).** He told us this not so we would become some kind of idealistic dreamers, but so our minds would not be overcome by the evil in the world.

I have always been careful not to watch upsetting newscasts or read articles that glamorized Satan's work. After I got saved, God showed me how TV programs breed fear in victims, too. So other than Christian TV and family-type movies, I watch very little secular programming.

Today, I continue to believe this is one key in keeping my mind and heart free of the tormenting root of fear.

Once as Dr. Lester Sumrall, pastor and founder of Feed the Hungry, was entering Smith Wigglesworth's home for a visit, he carried a newspaper. Wigglesworth, a world renowned evangelist, told him to leave the newspaper outside as he closely guarded his spirit from evil reports. I do read newspapers, but I do not read articles that I know will upset me. There are times I will not allow people to discuss Satan's hideous deeds.

You see, there is a difference between helping others work through tragic events of their lives and randomly discussing the heinous crimes Satan is responsible for. People sometimes ask, "How can you know what's going on if you isolate yourself from current events?" I do not live in a cave, but I do diligently guard my spirit from those things which promote fear.

One night, as I was watching Christian TV, God spoke through a young woman who had been controlled by fear. Her behavior was as mine had been — staying up all hours of the night, afraid of the unknown, immobilized from doing what she desired in her life.

She said God had given her Scripture that had set her free. **Hebrews 2:15** says Jesus came to **"deliver them who through**

fear of death were all their lifetime subject to bondage." The Holy Ghost spoke that Scripture into revelation knowledge in my heart. All my life, I had been afraid of death, afraid of those who could destroy my body. Once I had isolated the specific fear, it became much smaller and easier to combat with God's word.

Jesus had come to destroy the bondage. It was not future tense "Jesus will come." It was done when He came to Earth as a man, and through His physical death on Calvary, He destroyed the fear of death that the devil possessed.

Please study the following verses: **"Since the children have flesh and blood, He too shared in their humanity so that by His death He might destroy him who holds the power of death that is, the devil; and free those who all their lives were held in slavery by their fear of death." (Hebrews 2:14-15 NIV)**

Years earlier, when my teenage son was an infant, we lived in a small apartment above a jewelry store. I was finishing my bachelor's degree in business at a small college in rural Ohio. I lived in my little apartment and attended Bluffton College with the help of financial aid. Bluffton was a tiny college town with no crime to speak of. Yet, I was dragging the furniture near doors, staying up all night under the guise of studying. This was a few years before I became a Christian, so the spirit of fear was in full-blown operation.

My brother, a successful artist living in New York City, came to visit and asked me why I was so terrified. Living in crime-ridden New York, he could not fathom my paranoia in Bluffton, Ohio.

I told him I didn't know why I was so afraid, but I said, "What if someone breaks in and stabs me repeatedly with a knife?"

He said pragmatically, "Well then, you've spent your entire life being consumed with a fear of something that will be over in a matter of seconds."

Since I was a college senior, majoring in business, I could see the poor investment of time and energy I was making by being afraid of something that might never happen. I could see the imbalance, but since I did not have Christ's help, I couldn't change it.

But years later, when I saw the young woman on Christian TV who had been completely freed of fear, I told myself I could walk in an even greater level of freedom. I studied the second chapter of Hebrews for some time. I had identified that I was afraid of someone physically harming me. By this time, I was a student at Only Believe Ministries Bible College, and my mind was being transformed through consistent teaching.

Jesus had told us in **Matthew 10:28, "Fear not them which kill the body, but are not able to kill the soul, but rather fear him which is able to destroy both soul and body in hell."** God asks us in Isaiah 51 why should we be afraid of a man that shall die, and forget our Maker, who is always with us? Isaiah had a revelation of God as Jehovah Shammah, the God that is always near.

Isaiah had another revelation that God was going to free His children from the Babylonians. He was going to lead them out of their captivity, just as our Heavenly Father can free us from our self-made prisons.

The 40th through the 66th chapters of Isaiah speak of the freedom from exile and the soon-coming Messiah. I studied these later chapters of Isaiah for years. Over and over I read the forty-third chapter where the Lord says, **"Fear not, for I have redeemed you, I have called you by name; you are mine. When you pass through the waters, I will be with you; and when you pass through the rivers, they will not sweep over you: When you walk through the fire, you will not be burned, the flames will not set you ablaze."** (Isaiah 43:1&2 NIV)

I could not understand how God said He was there, and that He would be there, and that I would not be hurt. How could I give up protecting myself, when I felt He had allowed me to be hurt in the past?

One afternoon, I prayed with a precious saint who had been badly burned in a fire. As I held her hands, I was all too aware that she had no fingers. They had been literally burned off. To defy the devil, I guess, she always lit candles when she prayed. A little like saying, **"He that's in me is greater than you, devil."** 1 John 4:4

After we prayed, I wept for hours. I said, "See, God, you said in Isaiah that you would never let us be burned. Then where are her fingers?" I was so confused, I continued, "Where were you,

God, when I was hurt too, so many times, in so many ways?"

He spoke to me very softly and said, "It never touched your spirit."

For a brief moment I didn't understand, and then I realized there was a part of me that belonged solely to God. Paul writes **"though our outward man perish, yet the inward man is renewed day by day."** **(2 Corinthians 4:16)** We do not always understand God's plan, but we can be reassured by Romans 8:28 that He will make good out of every evil the devil brings to destroy us.

After that woman was burned, she required extensive treatment in a hospital. She saw the ineffectual and negligent treatment administered to alcoholics and addicts who came to the hospital's emergency room. Even in the midst of her pain, she used her background in counseling to help found a treatment center in that hospital for alcoholics and addicts.

For me, I decided to do as that pastor told me years ago on the psychiatric ward, when I was a patient. He said God had called me to help others who had been abused as I had been. I pray this day that there is some Scripture in this chapter that will help free you from living in fear.

Isaiah 42:7 prophesies of the Messiah who will come **"to bring out the prisoners from the prison."** He has come, and you have been set free from your prison of fear. Jesus is the key to your cell door.

I pray that as you study God's Word you will find the key to eternal freedom in Jesus' name.

CHAPTER FOUR

CONFIDENCE
through CHRIST

"I can do all things through Christ which strengtheneth me."
Philippians 4:13

In secular psychology, there is a type of behavior modification known as Rational Emotive Therapy.*1 In this type of therapy the patient tries to build self-esteem rationally through correction of the thought process. Most sexually and physically abused people have also been through continual verbal abuse. In some families the way to correct behavior is to tell the child, "You are stupid, bad, and ugly." Negative behavior will cease, but so will the ability for the child to see himself or herself in a positive perspective.

These negative thoughts literally become tapes that a person plays over and over in his or her mind, affecting self-esteem for the rest of their lives. Rational Emotive Therapy entails listing negative thoughts about oneself, then countering them with positive or correct thoughts.*2 Example: "You are so stupid, you will never get a good job." Correction: "I am an intelligent person, I will be a valuable asset to an employer."

People who have been conditioned to think negative thoughts about themselves will continually allow others to treat them in ways that are unacceptable to society, and unacceptable to God. Verbal abuse might not have occurred in the home of origin, but if a man or woman remains in a long-term abusive relationship, his or her self-esteem may be damaged in the same way. He or she will believe there is something wrong with them that causes others to victimize them.

A classic example involved a woman who had been beaten by

her husband and brought to a shelter for battered women. At this time, I had become a volunteer at the shelter to assist other battered wives and rape victims deal with their crises. I asked this woman if anything had preceded the violent episode. She said, "Yes, it was my fault."

As I looked at her blackened eye it was impossible to see how it could have been her fault, so I asked her to explain. She said, "I promised my husband that I would make spaghetti for dinner, but I went to the mall instead. I didn't have time to make the spaghetti so I had to make hamburgers. You can see that it was my fault."

I could see nothing of the sort. However, I could see that this woman honestly believed she was to blame for the beating. I was to see her on a crisis basis seven times following that meeting. During one of these meetings her six-year-old son became angry with her and savagely bit into her arm, leaving a gaping wound. He was being taught to be an abuser through visual and verbal imagery.

I was not, nor am I, a certified counselor. I contacted the director of the shelter and said I could not deal with this woman. She did not desire to change her life, she merely desired to have someone else view the battle scars of her tragic existence. A sad phenomenon of abuse is the attention it draws to the victim. When you have had little or no attention, Satan can trick you into believing even negative attention is really worth the cost.

Let's draw God into this picture. Rational Emotive Therapy can correct the thought process, but it will not heal the broken heart or mend the wounded spirit. This is why Jesus came to Earth.

When a person accepts Jesus as Lord and Savior, they become a **new creature; old things have passed away; behold, all things have become new." (2 Corinthians 5:17)** Yet, unless taught how to become a new creature, those with abusive backgrounds will never be who Christ intends them to be.

There is a great deal to be said for the necessity of deliverance at the altar. We must command not only the unclean spirit, but tormenting spirits such as addiction, depression, and suicide to loose their hold on those victimized, in Jesus' name.

We then get frustrated as a church when we do not see them

walking in the deliverance that Jesus purchased at Calvary. Laying on hands and commanding spirits out is not enough. We must teach those who have never been loved what love is. After all, it says in **I John 4:8**: **"God is love."** To teach victims to love, we must first teach them it is safe to share.

Often, a man or woman who was victimized will internalize the emotional pain and never tell anyone about the experience. Or at least they will not talk about the incident until they are no longer able to function due to the depression that arises from bottling their feelings.

When a person is initially abused, several things can happen. (Remember, each circumstance is different, so don't generalize or think you understand until the victim shares with you.) A child is often set up to be a victim by dysfunctional verbal conditioning in the home. When children are victimized the abuser often tells them no one will believe them, that it is their fault it happened, or threatens to hurt them or someone they love. Often a victim tells Mother or Father what Grandpa or Uncle did that was violating and they are not believed, or maybe they are believed, but the family is so dysfunctional the child is just told not to talk about it.

Sexual violation is heartbreaking, but the betrayal caused by the lack of reaction confirms in the victim's mind that he or she can never trust anyone. It verifies the fear that he or she is not important and that what has happened to them is of little consequence. The tragedy of this incident will literally destroy the inner core of one's ability to trust, to love, or to perceive truth.

Often, the one who should instill morals and values is the one who violates the child. This births a spirit of rejection and rebellion that will grow and dictate the child's behavior if left unchecked.

In 1986, I met a group of fellow victims who helped to change my life. I attended a local chapter of Adult Children of Alcoholics. The first night I came into the group, I was extremely depressed and desperate for help. I had been released from the psychiatric ward where I had given my life to Christ. Yet I was unable to view my life with any degree of hope.

Remember, the psychiatrist in charge had said that I would probably die in a mental institution. My track record was extremely bleak. Without a miracle his prognosis would have been inevitable.

Adult Children of Alcoholics is not only for those raised in alcoholic homes, but for those raised with any type of dysfunction. Although God used this group to help me, this is not a Christian organization. The third step of the ACOA program is "to turn your life and will over to God as you understand Him."*3

Unfortunately, most people I came in contact with in ACOA did not know the God of Abraham, Issac and Jacob. They did not know that Jesus, wholly God yet totally man, must be the Lord and Savior of your life through personal relationship. Nor did they know that God's precious Holy Spirit had been sent to this Earth as Jesus ascended into Heaven, to comfort and teach us all that we must know.

Yet the precious Holy Spirit led me to these meetings to begin my healing. At the time, I was unable to speak in front of a group, so I would sit hunched over, trying to be inconspicuous and listen. I had always felt alone, that my life was the only one spent in nightmare. But as I heard the devastating stories of other group members, I saw that I was not alone.

At the first meeting, I remember being amazed at the level of intelligence and character in the faces around that table. There were about thirty people at that meeting, and their smiles offered me hope. You see, there are stages of healing.

Emotional healing is no different than physical healing. If someone cuts you with a knife, first the wound bleeds. There is a healing and cleansing in that blood. It is much like the tears which at times must flow from our eyes. In **Psalm 56:8**, David says our tears are stored in a bottle. We must be willing to listen to those who have gone through personal tragedy — not only listen, but validate that their grief and pain are real.

We must let them cry and mourn for what they have lost. Then we must comfort them by explaining that God is able to miraculously give back all that the enemy has stolen.

Often, the church criticizes those who turn to secular psychology for help in overcoming the tragedies of their past. We label self-help groups and recovery seminars as crutches employed by weak Christians. Yet, we have offered no alternative means of overcoming the horror victims live with daily.

Instead those already wounded are forced to remain silent. As the broken-hearted try to share the hurts of their past, we tell them their answer lies in **"...forgetting those things which are behind, and reaching forth unto those things which are before." (Philippians 3:13)**

But Paul was not talking about forgetting hurtful things which almost destroyed him. The word "things" in Philippians 3:13 is originally derived from the Greek word **agathos** which means benefit or good. Paul was referring to forgetting the prestige he held as a blameless Pharisee, laying down his social and political power and position for the love of Christ. Please study Philippians 3:3-14 to understand Paul's decision to lay aside confidence in himself, and to accept his **Confidence through Christ.**

We must develop our own self-help groups within the church. Christian counselors need to look at the long-term effects of abuse and dysfunction. Techniques similar to Rational Emotive Therapy must be employed to teach people who they are in Christ.

We do not need to counter a negative thought with a positive thought. Rather, as we know the source of the negative thought is Satan, we must fight back with God's word. **Example**: negative thought, "You are so stupid, you will never get a job." **Correction:** "Devil, I rebuke you in Jesus' name, I have the mind of Christ Jesus, and He will supply my needs according to his riches in glory." (Philippians 2:5, 4:19)

For those who have lived through abuse, I will share a technique that helped me greatly. First, buy a small notepad that you can carry at all times. When Satan speaks a negative thought or lie to you about yourself, immediately stop what you are doing and write the thought down. If possible, write what God's word says, which is the truth about it. Here are several more examples that the devil uses on all of us:

Lie: No one loves me or cares what happens to me.

Truth: For long ago the Lord had said to Israel (His people): **"I have loved you with an everlasting love; I have drawn you with loving kindness." (Jeremiah 31:3 NIV)**

Lie: I can't do it, I'll never make it.

Truth: **"I can do all things through Christ which strengthens me." (Philippians 4:13 NKJ)**

Lie: I would be better off dead; there is no hope for me.

Truth: **"For I know the plans I have for you," declares the Lord. "Plans to prosper you and not to harm you, plans to give you hope and a future." (Jeremiah 29:11 NIV)**

There truly is hope through Jesus Christ, but we must train our minds to speak God's word. At first, you will recite His promises in an unsure way, but remember, **"Faith comes from hearing." (Romans 10:17 NIV)**

You must begin to tell yourself who you are in Jesus Christ. I know it is time-consuming to carry a notebook and write down the Devil's lies countered with God's truth. But how desperately do you want to be all that God wants you to be? After all, God says in Hebrews **11:6 "that He is a rewarder of those who diligently seek Him."** Satan has been lying to you all your life. Now it will take time to realize you are not a worthless mess, but truly you are the righteousness of God.

You will never be worthy or righteous because of anything you have or have not done. You are worthy and righteous simply because Christ shed His blood on Calvary as an atonement for your sin. Read and meditate on the following Scriptures:

"And He died for all, that those who live should no longer live for themselves but for Him who died for them and was raised again.

"So from now on we regard no one from a worldly point of view. Though we once regarded Christ in this way, we do so no longer. Therefore, if anyone is in Christ, he is a new creation; the old has gone, the new has come! All this is from God, who reconciled us to Himself through Christ and gave us the ministry of reconciliation: that God was reconciling the world to Himself in Christ, not counting men's sins against them. And He has committed to us the message of reconciliation. We are therefore Christ's ambassadors, as though God were making His appeal through us. We implore you on Christ's behalf: Be reconciled to God. God made Him who had no sin to be sin for

us, so that in Him we might become the righteousness of God."
(2 Cor. 5:15-21 NIV)

Please close this chapter by praying this prayer with me:

Father, please help me to see myself as You see me, a new creation through Jesus Christ. Break Satan's lying manipulative power over me and set me free through your word. As I study and meditate on those things that You say that I am, let me begin to believe in my heart as I confess only good about myself with my mouth.

I ask forgiveness for my wrongs of yesterday, and I receive that forgiveness by faith. I will not allow the Devil to remind me of who I was yesterday, rather I will remind him of who I am today through Christ. God, without You, I realize I can do nothing. But with **"Confidence through Christ,"** I can fulfill all the things you have called me to do. I truly thank you for the Holy Spirit's help in guiding me into revelation knowledge of who You are. As I get to know You, I will learn to know who I am through You. Your Son still bears the scars of Calvary, but His scars are healed and there is no pain. Lord, heal my wounds, and use my scars as a reminder of how much I've overcome through you in Jesus' precious name.

CHAPTER FIVE

RAGE

**(Including
SHAME-The Silencing Factor)**

AMAZING GRACE

Amazing grace how sweet the sound
that saved a wretch like me
I once was lost, but now I'm found
Was blind but now I see.

'Twas Grace that taught
my heart to fear
And grace my fears released
How precious did that grace appear
The hour I first believed.

John Newton (1779)

Twenty years ago, I graduated from high school. Well, actually I was awarded a diploma. I had spent most of my senior year in Toledo State Mental Hospital. After release from the hospital, I found a job as a waitress and a tiny apartment. I was barely 19, and I wanted to start my life anew. It was wonderful to be free. But then gradually, the demonic depression crept back into my life. I became unable to cope. The unclean spirit had been dormant for a time, then it became active again.

I was tormented almost continually by inner voices that were destructive and self-loathing. I remember standing in front of the bathroom mirror for long periods of time calling myself names and saying over and over, "I hate you, I hate you." There was also a driving force to hurt myself.

Several years before, I had found that there was great release from this demonic force if I would subject myself to physical pain. Some abuse victims become anorexic or bulimic (starving or purging), others participate in a form of masochistic behavior that includes self-mutilation, drug or sexual addiction. Once again, it is necessary to refer to the man at the tomb of the Gadareenes in **Mark 5:5**:

"And always, night and day, he was in the mountains, and in the tombs, crying and cutting himself with stones."

One morning, I did not go to my waitress job. Though I have no memory of the incident, my boss said I called, and said I was dead. My behavior had become increasingly erratic. A short time later, when I did not show up for work she became concerned and sent one of our regular customers to check on me.

When he entered my apartment (thank God I had not locked the door.) He found me in a pool of blood. He immediately called an ambulance. I fought viciously with the attendants. I did not understand why I was throwing lamps at them trying to keep them away. They quickly subdued me and took me to the emergency room.

I had repeatedly cut my left arm with a razor blade, and it had to be sewn back together. The emergency room doctor shook his head disgustedly and cursed at me. He said something about wasting his time on a teen-ager trying to take her life when he had a room full of people fighting for theirs.

I'm not sure if I was trying to take my life. I just felt compelled to cut myself. When he asked me why, I said with some confusion, "Because God told me to." I did not know how closely Satan can imitate the voice of our Beloved Father.

I am not sharing this demonic episode to glorify Satan. I am sharing that you might gain insight into the operation of the unclean spirit. In **Mark 5:5**, we read that **"night and day"** the demon-possessed man at the tombs was cutting himself and crying out.

For this poor possessed man there was no rest from the unclean spirit that tormented him. Twenty-four hours a day, the spirit's insatiable desire to destroy the man was in operation. Twenty-four hours a day the man at the tombs was controlled as an instrument of his own destruction.

I have been that man at the tombs. It took Jesus to set me free through Pastor Myers' prayer commanding the unclean spirit to leave me. Then the pastor taught me the Word, Scripture by Scripture, as described in the chapter on fear.

Brother Norvel Hayes says there are only two ways to scripturally cast out a devil. You must either command it to "come out" or "go," in Jesus' name.*1   Some educated, philosophical church people might shake their heads in disbelief. They don't believe demons exist today because they were never tormented by one.

Another example of this demonic form of rage occurred in my late teens. The rage inside me became so uncontrollable that the hospital staff had to strap me to a bed with leather restraints on my hands and feet for days at a time.

I was born with an idealistic perception of how the world should function. It was the unfairness of my circumstances that caused my cyclical bouts of uncontrollable anger, resulting in repeated hospitalizations, and ultimately leading to institutionalization.

Webster's Dictionary defines rage as a "violent and uncontrolled anger; fury; a fit of violent wrath."*2 Inside I was furious that I had never been allowed to be a child. Most people who have grown up in dysfunction understand that at a very early age they were required to care not only for their needs but for the needs of others.

The sexual abuse also destroyed girlhood dreams of innocence, and I was enraged that these atrocities had occurred.

One of the first steps to overcoming my rage began with the words spoken by a secular psychiatrist. This doctor had been on my case for several years. One night, I was admitted to the hospital in such a rage that it was once again necessary to strap me to the bed.

Most physicians and hospital workers are sympathetic toward those they treat. Unfortunately, they try to deal with what they call mental illness, and have little or more commonly no knowledge that Satan is real. Restraints are a last resort in controlling a patient, as they are extremely uncomfortable and dehumanizing.

The doctor was saddened that he had to repeatedly restrain me in such a fashion. The following day, seeing that the rage (unclean spirit) had subsided, he told the nurses to set me free. What he said next made me realize that I wasn't insane, as Satan had led me to believe.

"The person that's really sick never comes here. They are too ill to realize they need help," he said.

"The person that comes here is sane enough to realize that there is only craziness surrounding them," the doctor added.

By this time I had begun to view myself as an animal, one that needed to be tied to a bed with leather restraints. His words were like precious healing ointment. There was legitimate reason for my anger. I was not insane. I was sane enough to cry out at the injustice that had been done to me.

It is perhaps the small things that are taken from you due to sexual abuse as a child that cause the most anger. Most people take simple gestures of affection, like hugs and kisses, for granted. I was never to enjoy a hug or a kiss without wondering what the person was trying to take from me.

From my own experience, and from sharing with others who have been abused it is common that abuse is perpetrated by more than one victimizer. Quite often, if a child has been sexually abused, that child has had to fight advances from other adults. Satan has targeted the child after initially opening the door at the time of the first victimization.

When you counsel victims of abuse, you will find it is not uncommon for this phenomena to occur. I caution you to pass no judgment on the people you counsel. These people were not adults but children when these events occurred.

Satan controls victims with shame. That is how he silences them, keeping them from getting the help they need to change the situation. Satan also is adept at sending abusers to those already abused for their complete devastation. Many adults have been so ravaged by childhood victimization that they continue to lead lives of victims. **Shame** is the silencing factor that prevents dedicated Christians from leading the life of victory God intended.

When I was a young Christian, Satan used an evangelist I greatly respected to try to destroy me. This evangelist said something about me that was hurtful and untrue in front of hundreds of people. I was devastated. I had been spiritually raped, and I frantically thought of suicide.

God intervened and I was able to get counsel from my pastor. My pastor assured me that everyone present knew what had been said was untrue. He told me that ministers of God sometimes "miss it."

I couldn't believe I had been thinking of taking my life over an untrue statement. I asked Pastor Doseck why I wanted to hurt myself when others hurt me?

He said, "All your life people have controlled you with shame." He added, "You must know yourself, know who you are."

The undeserved shame we carry as victims causes us to react with rage towards ourselves and others. In the New Testament the word shame is often defined as disgrace.*3 **Disgrace is to be devoid or absent of God's grace.** Without grace we become powerless against the attacks of the enemy.

Jesus took our shame to the cross of Calvary according to **Hebrews 12:2, "Looking unto Jesus the author and finisher of our faith; who for the joy that was set before him endured the cross, despising the shame."** His blood purchased freedom not only from sin, but from shame. Now in exchange for our shame His righteousness is on us. **(2 Corinthians 5:21)**

Isaiah prophetically records Jesus suffering, **"I offered my back to those who beat me, my cheeks to those who pulled out my** beard; I did not hide my face from shame (mocking) and spitting. Because the Sovereign Lord helps me I will not be disgraced. Therefore I have set my face like a flint, and I know I will not be put to shame." (Isaiah 50:6&7 NIV)

In order to rekindle our shame consciousness the devil tries to strip us of who we are in Christ. Satan wants us to become spiritually, emotionally, and physically naked. **(Revelations 16:5)**

But God wants to give back all the enemy has taken from us. **Isaiah 61:7** gives us a promise from God concerning our shame. **"For your shame ye shall have <u>double</u>; and for confusion they shall rejoice in their portion: therefore in their land they shall possess the <u>double</u>: everlasting joy shall be unto them."** The word "double" in the original Hebrew text is from the word, **mishneh**, which is defined as **"twice as much."***4

For the shame Satan has caused we are entitled to twice as much of God's blessing. We must accept Christ's redemptive sacrifice for our shame by faith, rather than silently suffering.

This pattern of silence is no different with those who have been physically or verbally abused. Often, we let others treat us the way we are accustomed to being treated. At times there will be a cry from within our soul that will shout, "No more."

Years ago, I attended several meetings for spouses of alcoholic, addictive or abusive partners. One woman I never saw before that meeting or in all the years following made a great impact on me. Mates of violent spouses live in constant fear of physical danger. This woman looked at me as she said, "You don't leave them before they kill you, you leave them before you kill them."

The woman proceeded to tell us that 15 years earlier she had killed her young husband. She had been locked in a lifestyle of abuse. Her husband would get drunk, come home very late, and beat her. Her children were small and she felt she had no option except to tolerate the beatings.

But one night something inside of her broke. She could not bear to be abused again. This time when she heard his car pull in, she was waiting with a gun. She was sent to prison for several years. She wondered how to explain this to her youngest son, who had no memory of the events.

It was a small meeting; perhaps someone there was shocked. I don't think so, though. As life-long victims, most of us understood the breaking point of the rage that turns into violence. In my case the rage would most frequently be turned upon myself. Yet there were isolated times when I became like some raging animal, endangering those who crossed my path.

Once in my late teens, I methodically planned the gruesome murder of my abuser. I say gruesome because I had mentally orchestrated it. I had even selected the knife that I would plunge into his repugnant body as payment for his crimes. It was God's miraculous hand even then that spared me from committing this act. I was hospitalized before I could fulfill my plan.

This last decade has been a time of fascination with crimes of rage. Movies and television shows portray abused wives killing their husbands, or abused children murdering their abuser in a fit of rage. Headlines continue to be sprinkled with these kinds of crimes today.

To those of us who have lived with this demonic force of rage, these movies and headlines hold no fascination. We understand the all-consuming anger that causes a victim to break. Personally, I often weep when I hear of one of these cases. It reminds me how far I've come with Christ's delivering help.

No matter how unfair the past has been, Jesus Christ has the power to deliver you from the self-made prison of a life controlled by rage. If you find yourself angry for reasons you don't understand, or afraid of yourself, Christ can set you free.

Yet, throughout this book we refer to the price you must pay to be free. You must desire your freedom more than any of the negative rewards acting outside of God's will brings.

Last Sunday at church, I wept in gratitude as Christian musician Don Smithey shared his rendition of the classic hymn, "Amazing Grace." The music and theme of the hymn are beautiful, but that's not why I wept. I wept, remembering the poor tormented young woman I'd been almost 20 years earlier, locked in a tiny cell on an isolation ward of a Columbus hospital.

I had cut my hands with a glass vase that belonged to another patient. For my protection, the staff had been forced to put me in a small cold cell. Protective screen covered the window of the otherwise barren walls of the cell. A mattress on the floor was the only furnishing.

Before the nurse locked the heavy metal door of my prison, she handed me several thick phone directories, and told me to take my anger out on them. I tore pages out of the directories until my cell was knee-deep in wadded paper. Then the spirit tired of that game and began to rip the hospital garb that was my attire. Before I could stop myself, I was clawing the screen of that window with my poor cut hands. I was screaming in pain, and anguish, and anger.

I thought no one heard my screams for help. I sobbed until the rage was spent, and then I began to sing. I sang to block out the voice of the demonic spirit, and the pain of my aloneness. I had never read the Bible, so I didn't know that in the 16th chapter of Acts, Paul and Silas sang praises to God until the prison doors were opened, and their chains were loosed.

I huddled in the corner of the cell that was dark by now. The light had gone out as the sun had set. I pulled my knees into my chest, and wrapped my arms around my body for warmth, and I sang the songs I could remember. One of the songs was "Amazing Grace." I was not to realize for years how awesomely amazing God's grace really is — how a tormented girl could become a strong woman because of that grace.

That very night, I saw God's grace and mercy as an attendant appeared and said I was to be returned to my ward. There had been a reprieve. I looked down at the shredded clothes that barely covered my body, and knew it was not due to good behavior on my part. The reason for my release was that the other patients on the ward had banded together and started a hunger strike to protest my transfer to isolation. They had refused to eat until I was set free.

I was overcome that they cared enough for me to give up their food. Most of the other patients on that psychiatric ward were victims, too. It was almost Christmas. We had worked together to decorate the ward with bells, and reindeer, and tinsel galore. Late that night as I was escorted back to the ward, there was a cheer of victory.

Besides mental torment, rage can cause physical problems. Many of those I met in mental wards suffered from diverse physical ailments. By the time I was 19, I had developed an acute case of ulcers. For six weeks, I could eat no food, just medication and milk products. For years, I experienced debilitating headaches.

Many abuse victims become hypochondriacs. We receive attention when we are ill. When we're sick, people are nicer to us and do not expect as much from us. Unfortunately, those around us quickly tire of hearing about our maladies.

We hurt ourselves because we have been hurt. We do not treat our bodies as God intended. We abuse them just as we abuse our emotions. After all, we can't be worth much if God allowed all these horrible things to happen to us. Or can we?

To answer this question, I need to tell the story of a beautiful woman I met recently. To protect her identity, I will call this courageous woman "Melissa."

Melissa was a relatively new convert to Christianity. She was struggling to overcome the victimization from her past. Satan didn't like it, and he set a trap to destroy her.

A man she did not know attacked and raped her in her apartment, as her little daughter slept. I asked her, "How do you deal with the rage that a violent act like rape creates?" Remember, she already was trying to deal with past abuses.

She sat pensive for a time. Then she said God had shown her mental pictures of hurtful incidents in her past. As He showed her the pictures, He spoke quite simply and said in a still small voice, "I was there."

"I know what you mean," I said excitedly. "God did that same thing for me as He was healing me."

I remembered the time I stood in the midst of the praise and worship service in a small church, and suddenly I saw myself as a teen-ager walking down the long corridor of the state mental institution. I vividly saw the dress and black tights that clung to my emaciated body. I would refuse to eat for weeks at a time, hoping to speed my death.

I recoiled as I saw the picture of that poor defenseless teen-ager in that horrible place. I was about to rebuke Satan for showing me that ugly memory, when a gentle voice spoke from deep within. The voice full of compassion and love said simply, "I was there."

Another time I saw a picture of myself desperately trying to break free of the leather restraints that tied me to my hospital bed. I remembered the frustration and panic I experienced as I realized I could not free myself. I looked like an animal writhing in pain caught in a trap. Again the gentle voice of our heavenly Father said, "I was there."

Over and over, God has shown me painful pictures and said, "I was there." He was not just saying, "I was there." Embodied in the compassion of His voice were the words, "It hurt me to see you suffer so."

I know today that it hurt our dear Lord more than it hurt me. The only difference was that God already had seen the end from the beginning. **(Isaiah 46:10)** He did not want me to experience all those hideous things, but since I had He could cause good to come from the evil.

For me the good that has come is a great desire to help those still bound by chains and fetters. As stated earlier, rage is the result of the victim's reaction to the unfairness of the circumstance. The rage can be dissipated only by validating that the victim has a right to be angry at the unrighteous acts Satan is responsible for. Jesus himself became righteously angry that men used His Father's temple as a place to change money.

Once you acknowledge that someone has suffered a terrible injustice, it is necessary to teach him or her the art of forgiveness. Forgiveness is a divine gift that can be acquired by decision and prayer, coupled with instruction in God's word. The following chapter on forgiveness will look at ways God has appointed to deal with our hurt. For many of us, the violations that have occurred cannot humanly be forgiven. Thank God that He is not human. He can actually help us to walk in a supernatural level of forgiveness. Once we begin to seek this ability to forgive, we will see that our rage no longer has the same hold on our emotions.

There is another step to curing rage that is often overlooked. Quite simply, we must learn to treat our bodies as God intended. We must exercise on a regular basis, and eat foods that ensure good health. Most children of dysfunction are told they have a chemical imbalance. I was told my imbalance could be controlled only through heavy medication. Praise God, I've had no medication in years, but I have had a regulated diet with physical exercise. Maybe you're thinking that diet and exercise can't be that important. Victims who are prone to fits of rage need to be delivered. Then they must maintain a lifestyle that avoids all excesses. Even extreme stress and tiredness can bring on the rage. You must tell others when you are overburdened. You must learn to say no to activities that exhaust you. You must learn to take time to engage in positive spiritual and physical behaviors.

When the unfairness of life reignites the spirit of rage, there is one more picture God usually shows me. It is the image of Jesus dying on the cross. He could have been so angry that He would have refused to fulfill the Father's plan. Instead He gave the ultimate sacrifice, His life.

May the peace purchased through His shed blood replace the rage that, for some, has been a constant companion. May the double portion of blessing remove your shame. In Christ's precious name, may you be freed of the anger that can destroy the spirit, soul, and body.

CHAPTER 6

FORGIVENESS

So Jesus answered and said to them, "Have faith in God. For assuredly, I say to you, whoever says to this mountain, Be removed and be cast into the sea, and does not doubt in his heart, but believes that those things he says will come to pass, he will have whatever he says. Therefore I say to you, whatever things you ask when you pray, believe that you receive them, and you will have them. And whenever you stand praying, if you have anything against anyone, forgive him, that your Father may also forgive you your trespasses. But if you do not forgive, neither will your Father in heaven forgive your trespasses." (Mark 11: 22-26 NKJ)

It was Christmas Eve 1980. Before darkness settled, beckoning the day we celebrate the birth of our precious Savior, the shelter filled to capacity. I was 26 years old, nine months pregnant, and had been a resident of the shelter for almost two months. I had seen women come and go, but I was not prepared for the onslaught of battered women that Christmas Eve.

I sat in a large overstuffed chair in the living room staring at a gaily decorated Christmas tree. Frightened mothers and their children huddled close together on the living room floor. They had all arrived that day as emergency situations, and there were no beds available. We made them beds on the floor, of blankets and donated bedding, and we were glad for safety and warmth. Yet in each of our hearts was the dismal hopelessness that victims of abuse carry through their lives.

I am reminded of the story so long ago of our dear Jesus. On the night of his birth, he, too, had no bed to lie upon. I did not know about the love of Jesus then. I did not know that He suffers as we suffer. " **For we do not have a High Priest who cannot be touched with the feeling of our infirmities. . . " (Hebrews 4:15)** Jesus is our High Priest, and He feels what we feel. The word **"infirmities"** in the Greek actually refers to our **weaknesses.**[*1] Jesus not only feels the suffering in our bodies, but His heart breaks as our hearts break.

As I looked upon the faces of the children asleep on the floor, my soul cried out to a God I did not know. I saw the little girl who had been beaten with a coat hanger by her father, and her older sister who had been raped and ravaged far beyond her adolescent years. Their mother, thin as a Holocaust victim, slept on the floor with her five children.

The baby boy in the white bassinet in the corner of the room confused me most. Ugly green bruises in the shape of a man's hand covered his face and neck. His father had gotten angry at the small infant's cries and had flung him against the wall, fracturing his skull and breaking his pelvis. The bruises did not confuse me; I had become hardened to them after being a resident awhile. What confused me was that the little baby boy named Jason, smiled as close to an angel's smile as I have ever seen.

Jason's mother defended the abusive father, who had once killed her dog to punish her. After a few months at the shelter, she went home to her husband, taking Jason with her. I wonder now, almost 15 years later, dear God, did Jason survive? If he did, at what cost?

I sat in my chair that Christmas Eve night, looking down at my large overdue belly, wondering what kind of world I was bringing my child into. What kind of life could I give him? I desperately wanted his existence to be better than mine. As I cried out to a God I had no relationship with, for a moment time stood still. A photograph of that scene was imbedded in my subconscious. At that moment I felt a peace I did not understand. I knew that some-one far greater than I could comprehend cared about each one of us in that crowded room.

Two weeks later, the director of the shelter coached me as I gave birth to my son. He was the first baby that had ever been born to a resident of the facility. New life brings a ray of hope into even the darkest situations. The women of the shelter had become my family. They heralded in the birth of my son, Zachary, as the angels heralded the birth of our Savior. The name Zachary means "the Lord remembers." The Lord remembered me when I didn't know Him. The Lord gave me my son, to give me a desire to live. He knew I was not well enough to desire to get better for myself.

Only those who have been victims understand the self-loathing that accompanies abuse. Once we have been abused in some way, whether verbal, emotional or physical, we begin to abuse ourselves. Unfounded self-hatred follows us our entire life without the rev-elation of Jesus' love.

I had established a rapport with the people at the shelter. After finding a government-subsidized apartment, I began volunteering there. I participated in emergency phone counseling with victims of domestic violence and rape. Unfortunately, I saw a spirit that invaded this work. It is what I call the "man-hater" spirit. Abuse becomes so pervasive that women band together to fight men.

The enemy is not the man or woman who victimized you. The enemy is not even a human being. The enemy is the devil. **" For our struggle is not against flesh and blood, but against the rul-**

ers, against the authorities, against the powers of this dark world . . ." (Ephesians 6:12 NIV)

The enemy is the demonic power that pornography possesses, causing a father to molest his daughter. The enemy is the addictive power of alcohol, causing a husband to blacken his wife's eye.

Another enemy often accompanies abuse, too. It is ignorance. The prophet Hosea told us that God said, **"My People are destroyed for lack of knowledge." (Hosea 4:6)** Ingrained behavior is learned behavior. When we are shown life lessons the wrong way, we develop wrong behavior. Children do not only learn what they are told; they learn what they see.

Let's look at Exodus 34:7 to begin to understand the importance of learned behavior in explaining the generational curse. Remember God is describing His own character in this Scripture. **"Keeping mercy for thousands, forgiving iniquity and transgression and sin, by no means clearing the guilty, visiting the iniquity of the fathers upon the children and the children's children to the third and fourth generation." (Exodus 34:7 NKJ)**

For centuries, believers have portrayed God as a wrathful avenger of sin, punishing generations for the sins of the father. Exodus 34:7 refers to the **iniquity** defined as **weakness**, **sin or perversity** of the original sinner,*(2) such as Adam, causing succeeding generations to suffer as well. It is not that God desires us to suffer. He desires to heal and restore us.

Sin activates a curse which results in poverty, sickness (physical or emotional) and spiritual death. But the great news, according to **Galatians 3:13, is that Jesus Christ set us free from the curse when He hung on that tree at Calvary.** There will be great emotional suffering if a child is abused. But through Christ we have a legal right to be freed of that suffering.

In the chapter, CONFIDENCE THROUGH CHRIST, I related a story of a woman being abused by her husband, whose small son began abusing her, too. From abuse we learn to abuse. We must desire to be set free of the cycle of abuse. Being a victim carries some rewards that we must be willing to relinquish.

For years, I wore my victimization like a badge. I nursed it, stroked it, and found great comfort in the fact that I had a reason for being "such a mess." According to psychiatric diagnosis, I had been permanently emotionally scarred and my life would be a very limited one. Whenever I failed at something, I blamed my past. The truth was, most often, I exerted little effort.

Myriads of people will comfort you by agreeing that you've been dealt a rotten hand in life, that they were dealt a rotten hand, too. According to them, you might as well take another tranquilizer and be grateful you are damaged enough to collect welfare, food stamps and live in subsidized housing. Then you can sit around all day watching soap operas and blame others for what has happened to you.

The devil almost trapped me in such a lifestyle. I spent two years on welfare when my son was a baby. I saw firsthand how demoralizing the system can be. While I was on welfare, I finished college, so I had hope that it would be a temporary situation. But I saw so many people frozen in welfare lines, who had been there for years and are probably still there. They had accepted the lie that this was their lot in life, and that it was someone else's fault.

The people who victimized you will be judged for those deeds when they stand before our Lord. It is useless to blame them. They are bound by Satan. Jesus gave us a remedy to free us from our unforgiveness. Jesus said, **" . . . Love your enemies, do good to those who hate you, bless those who curse you, and PRAY FOR THOSE WHO SPITEFULLY USE YOU "** (Luke 6:27-28 NKJ)

For almost a year after I established a personal relationship with Jesus Christ, my prayers were still hindered. I saw and felt the goodness of God all around me, yet, I was not walking in the victory of answered prayer. I continued to make poor life choices which had nothing to do with God's perfect will.

I began to seek God concerning my lack of manifestation of those things for which I petitioned. Very early in my study of the Bible, I found **Mark 11:23: " For assuredly, I say to you, whoever says to this mountain, Be removed and be cast into the**

**sea, and does not doubt in his heart, but believes that those
things he says will come to pass, he will have whatever he says."**

I came to believe this passage with my whole being. You see,
the Lord had eroded my mountain of emotional pain. He cast into
the sea, the hopelessness, that had been my life long companion.
In my spirit, I knew there was much more God wanted to do, but
something was holding me back. Then one day as I was reading
my Bible Mark 11:25 jumped off the page at me. **"And whenever you stand praying, if you have anything against anyone,
forgive him, that your Father in heaven may also forgive you
your trespasses." Mark 11:25 NKJ**

Instantly, I knew God was saying, "Unforgiveness is your problem." I was shocked at this revelation. I truly thought I had forgiven. I knew God required it of me. I knew not to speak evil of
others. I had even mouthed my forgiveness many times. Yet I
knew the Father's voice, and He had said I had not forgiven.

At the time, my pastor Peter Doseck was preaching a sermon
concerning forgiveness. It seemed as if the Holy Spirit had Pastor
stop and look directly at me and say, "If you have truly forgiven
somebody, you won't be irritated every time someone mentions
their name."*3 I had to admit there were people in my past whose
names I could not bear to hear. I saw the bitterness in my heart
when I would hear that they had been blessed in some way. A part
of me always wanted to say, "But you don't know what they've
done to me." Another facet of unforgiveness that I began to identify at that time was fear. I was afraid if I totally released people
for tragic things they had been a part of in my life, I would have to
allow them to come back into my life.

Once I pinpointed that I was afraid to totally forgive for fear
people who had once abused me would again gain control over
me, I sought God's help. He led me to a young Catholic priest,
who was also a counselor. Although I spoke to this man only
three times, he said something which freed me of the fear. He
said, "Do you remember the man who shot the pope?"

I emphatically said, "Yes." I had been horrified when I heard
someone had tried to kill the pope. He said, "Did you know the
pope went in to that prison and told the man I forgive you in the

name of Jesus Christ? But, the pope didn't tell the prison officials to let the man out."

That story provided the analogy that allowed me to see how forgiveness works. Just because you forgive someone does not negate that person's accountability for what he has done.

In Scripture Jesus tells us, **"Behold, I send you out as sheep in the midst of wolves. Therefore be wise as serpents and harmless as doves." (Matthew 10:16 NKJ)** The church has greatly lacked wisdom with regard to abuse victims. They have been told to remain in the situation and pray that it will change. People's lives have been ravaged because of the denial and inability the church has to counsel.

Once, I was in a church visiting and the pastor stood up and asked people to pray for a 5-year-old girl who was being sexually abused by her father. He asked that God would work on the father's heart and restore the family. I was as shocked as that pastor was when I walked to the front and asked if I could speak. He was so surprised, I think he handed me his microphone without thinking or maybe he saw the determination on my face.

As I looked out upon that congregation of several hundred people, I said, "Mama, I don't know where you are out there, but if your 5-year-old daughter is being abused, it's your responsibility to help her. Get her out of that situation now."

As the people stared at me, I continued, "It's your responsibility, too. If you call yourself Christians and know a child that's being abused and do not help them you will be held accountable. My life was almost destroyed because of sexual abuse. Praying is wonderful, but get the child safe and then pray."

Needless to say, no one commended me for my brief sermon, nor did they ask me to come back for a visit. But I'm glad I was there that day. I have come to realize that most Christians have no idea what abuse does to destroy a person. Therefore they have little wisdom to counsel its victims.

We as a church have thought forgiving someone means inviting the abuser back into your life. This is invalid. You might forgive someone for abusing you, but it doesn't mean you must include them in your tomorrows. Only God can judge true forgiveness. It is the condition of the heart He sees.

Only our heavenly Father can restore relationships that have been destroyed by violence, sexual perversion, or verbal battering. However, He will not allow His children to be destroyed by such relationships. God is the only one who can enable us to forgive that which is otherwise humanly impossible to forgive.

Sometimes, we have the greatest difficulty forgiving ourselves. Many victims of abuse have abused younger siblings or relatives as a result of their own abuse. I have seen the guilt of this childhood sin torment dedicated believers. In order to be freed of this guilt, we must accept by faith the work of redemption of Christ's suffering. Satan will deceive even the elect that total forgiveness was purchased at Calvary.

In **Isaiah 55:8** we are told **God's thoughts are not our thoughts**. When Isaiah was speaking of God's thoughts and ways, he was referring to God's viewpoint of forgiveness.

"Seek the Lord while He may be found. Call upon Him while He is near. Let the wicked forsake his way, and the unrighteous his thoughts; Let him return to the Lord, And He will have mercy on him, And to our God, For He will abundantly pardon. For my thoughts are not your thoughts nor are your ways my ways, says the Lord. "For as the heavens are higher than the earth so are my ways higher than your ways, and my thoughts than your thoughts."

(Isaiah 55:6-9 NKJ)

First, we must be freed of the fear that by forgiving, we are willing to permit ourselves or those we love to be abused again. Second, we must begin to understand that we as human beings do not possess the capacity to forgive. We are not able to forgive those who have wounded us deeply without God's mercy and grace on our behalf. Forgiveness is a divine process. It can be attained only through diligent search.

Our search for forgiveness must begin in God's throne room through prayer. In **Hebrews 4:16**, God's Word tells us **to "come boldly to the throne of grace, that we may obtain mercy, and find grace to help in time of need."** As we pray God will send us His grace, which is His ability to do what we are unable to do. If we desire God's mercy, we must pray to be merciful to others.

I began to pray in earnest that God would teach me to forgive those who had abused me. I also began to pray for those Satan had used to try to destroy me. I prayed most of all for their salvation, so that they could be freed from the Wicked One destroying their lives. At first, my prayers were labored and insincere. But as I continued, the Holy Spirit took over and I began to pray in earnest for those I called "enemies."

I began to see the Church's lack of understanding concerning forgiveness. People are forced to mouth words of forgiveness then told it will be all right. Often they still feel anger and bitterness lodged in their hearts. Then they begin to feel ashamed and condemned that they have not achieved forgiveness .

You can't forgive, but God can forgive through you. Ask someone who is non-judgmental to stand in prayer with you that forgiveness will manifest in your life.

For more than a year I prayed for the gift of forgiveness, then one day it unexpectedly arrived. I remember so vividly. I was turning the doorknob to enter my small apartment when it came. I stopped abruptly as I felt a horrible burden lift from me, then I was overcome with a feeling of love I'd never known. One by one, I thought of those who had hurt me, and I saw how insignificant the hurt was in the face of God's love.

I thought of the years of ulcers and migraine headaches, and I knew that as the unforgiveness had gone, the stomach problems and headaches had gone as well. I realized that I needed to learn to walk in the delivering power that I'd felt that day. It is prayer that has kept unforgiveness from resurfacing in my life. Prayer not only for myself, but continued prayer for those who wronged me yesterday and today. I also believe in the power of fasting to break the spirit of unforgiveness, but fasting only as God ordains.

My prayers are no longer hindered. They truly produce manifestation of God's provision. God has said He will meet all our needs in Philippians 4:19. You need to forgive in order to be God's best. Begin to pray and diligently seek the Lord concerning forgiveness. Only He can show you the path you must take through the wilderness. Begin by saying this prayer aloud:

Dear Lord,

I am not able to forgive, but you are. Please teach me, Lord, how to lay my hurts at the feet of Jesus Christ. Help me to allow those who have hurt me to no longer have control over me. Show me how to let go of my pain and bitterness by faith.

Lord, I pray for those who have abused me. (Say their names out loud.) I pray you will lead them to salvation. Father, bind Satan over their lives and set them free through the cleansing blood of Jesus.

Lord, help me to not look back and nurse my wounds, but help me to offer my wounds to you for healing.

Father, I need your mercy and grace as I am not able to walk in freedom without your help. I forgive, and I am forgiven this day. Now, help me to be diligent in seeking you. Teach me your ways and divinely implant your thoughts so that I can go on with you, free of my yesterdays.

Thank you, too, that as I forgive I will begin to see the answers to my prayers. Mountains will be moved on my behalf, and those things which I say in prayer will come to pass in Jesus' name.

AMEN

CHAPTER SEVEN

LOVE, ADDICTION, AND RELATIONSHIPS

HOW DO I LOVE THEE?

How do I love thee? Let me count the ways.
I love thee to the depth and breadth and height
My soul can reach, when feeling out of sight
For the ends of Being and ideal Grace.
I love thee to the level of every day's
Most quiet need, by sun and candle-light.
I love thee freely, as men strive for right;
I love thee purely, as they turn from praise.
I love thee with the passion put to use
In my old griefs, and with my childhood's faith.
I love thee with a love I seemed to lose
With my lost saints.
I love thee with the breath,
Smiles, tears, of all my life
    and, if God but choose
I shall but love thee better after death.

Elizabeth Barrett Browning

One of the greatest tragedies of dysfunction, particularly by sexual abuse, is the inability to have or sustain relationships. Yet many who are sexually abused do maintain long-term relationships. Why are some victims damaged in this area, and others relatively unharmed?

First, we must consider the role of the abuser. When the abuser is also the father or mother, the morals and values that should have been taught are not only destroyed, but actual infidelity in marriage is taught by the abuser. Remember we are discussing a spiritual battle. I believe the unclean spirit is often transmitted at the time of the initial sexual encounter.

We think of rape as sexual abuse, but **sexual abuse is any unwanted or unsolicited sexual advance that is inappropriately directed toward another.** A father kissing his daughter passionately instead of platonically, a lewd remark, or molestation (fondling of the private parts of another without consent), etc., all constitute sexual abuse.

Abuse and dysfunction affect people in very different ways depending on their ability to resolve crises. God did not create us to be "carbon copies" of each other. God has gifted some of us in areas to be an asset to our brothers and sisters.

Unfortunately, the same gifts that cause us to be sensitive to the needs of others can cause us to be overly sensitive in life. Our gift becomes a burden when we are not taught how to operate in it.

In an earlier chapter, "Confidence Through Christ," we discussed how children are often controlled in dysfunctional homes by negative verbal conditioning. "You're stupid, you're bad, you're ugly" will often stop unwanted behavior, but these words can also irreparably damage confidence. This type of conditioning creates a spirit of self-condemnation. An individual sets standards for himself, either so high that there is no way to attain the goal, or so low that little effort is required to achieve it. In other words, the person begins to see himself as a <u>loser</u>.

I met a precious young man who had recently been released from a psychiatric ward. He was obviously tormented, struggling with living, afraid of dying. He began to share with me when he sensed that I loved him with Christ's love and I desired to help him. He had been molested by an older female relative as a young boy. Victims of sexual abuse will often try to figure out what your "angle" is, what you're trying to take from them, as they have been robbed of their most valuable possession at an early age, themselves. It is difficult for them to understand that someone can love them simply for who they are.

Often, they will try to entice or seduce those who try to help them in order to prove that people are all alike. A wise pastor or counselor will recognize this seducing spirit can be operative at all times.

This man had paired up with a young woman who had been sexually abused by a relative as a child. The young couple fueled one another's sickness. The familiar spirit gained access through their shared rage and unforgiveness. The young man told me he led a very promiscuous life and by his mid-twenties, he had slept with more than one hundred women. "I can't stand them," he spewed angrily. Once he had sex with them, he said, they became disgusting to him.

Then he looked at the young woman and said, "But you don't make me feel that way."

But sad to say, she probably will make him feel that way. **"The wages of sin is death."** **(Romans 6:23)** Sex outside marriage always activates a type of death in our lives. This type of loathing goes even deeper. Those brought up to condemn themselves will loathe those who fall in love with them. Because they see themselves as no good, anyone who loves them becomes no good, too. The spirit of self-condemnation is often accompanied by a critical spirit that destroys not only the individual, but anyone who cares for them.

ADDICTION VERSUS LOVE

Often, a victim will team up with a victimizer. The night my son was born, the director of the shelter for battered women, Rochelle Twining, held my hand and helped me to bring him into the world. She tried to remain professional with clients. Yet, when someone holds your hand while your baby is born, you can't help but get close. Several months later when Rochelle said, "If there were 500 great men in a room and one jerk, you would walk right up to the jerk and say, "Here I am." I was confused at her callous attitude as I considered her my friend. Her remark stung like a slap on my face.

Later when I began volunteering at the shelter, I found out why Rochelle seemed to be distressed at times. When you see women and children beaten on a daily basis, you start to see men as the enemy.

Satan hides behind whatever camouflage he can. He always wants us to begin fighting people. He does not want us to recognize our true enemy.

Rochelle Twining, director of that shelter, estimated that about 90 percent of abused women return to the abusive situation within a short period of time.*1 Why would someone go back into a home where they know they will be beaten? Is it love? No, unfortunately, it's addiction. Is this kind of relationship acceptable to God?

Let's look at the fourth chapter of the book of John, beginning with the sixth verse: **"Now Jacob's well was there. Jesus therefore, being wearied from His journey, sat thus by the well. It was about the sixth hour. A woman of Samaria came to draw water. Jesus said to her, 'Give me a drink.' For His disciples had gone away into the city to buy food. Then the woman of Samaria said to Him, 'How is it that you, being a Jew, ask a drink from me, a Samaritan woman?' For Jews have no dealings with Samaritans. Jesus answered and said to her, 'If you knew the gift of God, and who it is who says to you, Give me a drink, you would have asked Him, and He would have given you living water.' The woman said to Him, 'Sir, you have nothing to draw with, and the well is deep. Where then do you get that living water? Are you greater than our father Jacob, who gave us the well and drank from it himself, as well as his sons and his livestock?' Jesus answered and said to her,**

'Whoever drinks of this water will thirst again, but whoever drinks of the water that I shall give him will never thirst. But the water that I shall give him will become in him a fountain of water springing up into everlasting life.' The woman

said to Him, 'Sir, give me this water, that I may not thirst, nor come here to draw.' Jesus said to her, 'Go call your husband and come here.' The woman answered and said, 'I have no husband.'

Jesus said to her, 'You have well said, I have no husband, for you have had five husbands, and the one whom you now have is not your husband; in that you spoke truly." John 4:6-18 NKJ

In this passage, we find Jesus, weary from his journey, resting at Jacob's well. A woman from Samaria comes along and Jesus asks her for a drink. Jesus asked her to satisfy his thirst, for He saw the consuming thirst within her. He knew she had great desire to satisfy her thirst for relationship. She was parched and dry from seeking love, and Jesus knew it. That is why He told her to go get her husband. But the woman said, "I have no husband."

Jesus said, **"for you have had five husbands, and the one whom you now have is not your husband; in that you spoke truly." John 4:18 NKJ.**

Jesus recognized that the woman had had five husbands. He did not say you have had one husband and lived illicitly with five other men. Apparently though, the last man the Samaritan woman was living with was not a husband.

Now, here we as a church begin to pick up stones and throw them at people. Jesus did not throw a stone, and He is the only one who could. Jesus knew no sin. He could have looked at the woman and said, "You wretched sinner." Instead, He told her revelation knowledge about how to worship God. He knew God would satisfy her, and that a spiritual relationship would give the Samaritan woman what she longed for.

Later, in **John 4:27**, we read that when His disciples came back, they "marveled" that Jesus talked with this woman. The disciples did not see this woman as a candidate for salvation. Yet, this woman not only gave her life to Jesus, she was the first woman preacher Scripture reveals. She went into the city and told the men they must come see the Christ.

How many of us have observed a young woman or man living a life of rampant sin, and have neglected to tell them about the living waters that Christ has? Have we been like the disciples and wondered what Jesus could possibly want with an unholy Samaritan? Perhaps God sees a preacher in that person just like the woman at the well.

There is a desperation that comes to those thirsty for relationship. They search for someone to make them whole, to make them complete or happy within themselves. This will never happen. It is impossible to make another person whole, complete or happy. We must be complete within ourselves through the sufficiency of Christ before we can ever truly be beneficial to another person. We live in a society and a generation of "What can you do for me?" God created us to serve and to think what we can do for others.

We see the greatest toll on relationships not only from dysfunction, but also from the "me" generation. We must not judge people who are selfish and unwilling to sacrifice to have relationship. We must teach them how to have relationship.

Recently, I went to my favorite Chinese restaurant for supper with a family I have been friends with for years. The food was so heavenly that I couldn't have believed anything could make it taste bad. But the dinner conversation nearly spoiled the meal.

The family began talking about someone they had known long ago. The sister said, "I heard she married for the third time." The brother smiled and said, "The third time is a charm." Then they went on to poke fun at someone who had married twenty-one times. They laughed and were having a bit of good-natured fun.

My heart was broken. I could only imagine how desperate someone must be to obtain love that they would marry twenty-one times, and still — without Christ — they would come up short.

The statement that the director of the shelter had made years ago sounded loudly in my ears that evening. "There could be 500 great men in a room and one jerk and you would walk up to that jerk and say, Here I am." Sometimes when a caustic remark wounds deeply, it is because it has truth buried within. The shelter's director had been right about me, and all those like me. We choose life partners unaware that they will ultimately try to destroy us.

There was an intake form we were required to fill out when entering the shelter. One question asked if there had been sexual abuse in your life as a child. Not coincidentally, 90 percent of the women had experienced sexual abuse as a child, and 90 percent returned to their abuser to be battered again.*2

Most of us at that shelter were never taught what love was as a child. We had heard the word love, but what we had seen spoke far louder than words. We had seen parents who said they loved each other literally fight like animals. We had seen bruises, heard screams, and often found ourselves caught in the crossfire. Then oddly enough, following an episode of abuse, there would be a period of reconciliation — what we at the shelter referred to as the honeymoon period.

During this honeymoon period, those who have fought viciously will be consumed with an insatiable lust for one another. How can this happen? Remember one's level of intelligence, social standing or career, have little to do with being a victim. Domestic violence and sexual abuse, like every other type of dysfunction, cross all socioeconomic backgrounds. Why? Because addiction is not limited to those of any specific class.

Just as some children are taught to love, many are taught to be addicted. Once I heard a member of Alcoholics Anonymous say that people become addicted to "people, places and things." When you grow up in the midst of continual crisis, you become addicted to crisis and to the people who create the crisis. Crisis becomes an emotional drug that you cannot live without.

In the book of Matthew, Jesus tells us, **"Give not that which is holy unto the dogs, neither cast ye your pearls before swine lest they trample them under their feet and turn and rend you." (Matthew 7:6)**

What was Jesus talking about? In the preceding verses Jesus tells us to judge not, concerning the faults of our brothers. He says, **"Give not that which is holy unto dogs."** Jesus was talking about people; dogs were literally Gentiles, the unsaved, non-Jewish of his day. Pigs in Scripture were regarded as a highly undesirable, unclean animal.

Jesus was warning us away from those who are not our brothers, from those operating in demonic activity, for they will destroy us.

Some years ago, when I was in the process of divorce, a Christian lawyer shook his head and said sadly, "Christina, you have no idea what love is. I don't think you ever will," he added. He knew me well and was aware of the sexual abuse, suicide attempts, hospitalizations, and the abusive marriage that were part of my history. His statement made me extremely angry. It made me feel hopeless and inferior. That dear friend was a wonderful Christian man, but he did not remember that at Calvary Jesus had purchased my deliverance and restored by ability to love.

At that time, I was a baby Christian with almost no understanding of God's word. I did however have a very real ability to hear God's voice. When God truly speaks it is as if time stands still. God literally marks the spot. As I stood on a river bank, brokenhearted by the faithlessness of my husband, in the midst of divorce, God spoke quite clearly, "You are not to date." This word spoken in the still small voice from within had no relevance to me. I could not imagine how I was going to be able to live. So, dating was not my most critical need.

For the first time in my life, I was totally alone. It was God and me. God began working on me from the inside out. It says in **Proverbs 3:12**, **"The Lord disciplines those he loves, as a father the son he delights in." (NIV)** I had spent a great deal of time and energy blaming other people for who I was. I blamed my parents for what I had not accomplished in my life.

Yet, in **Psalm 27:10** it says, **"When my father and my mother forsake me, then the Lord will take me up."** However, a child does see a parent as a role model. If their earthly father or mother has portrayed a perverted image, they will incorporate that into a distorted self-image. They will be unable to see God in the light of a perfect parent, who only desires good for his children.

It is important to understand why it is so difficult for some people to relate to the idea of a loving father. Some children are raised in a home where the father comes home after a night of drinking and begins breaking chairs, pictures, and anything that gets in his way. They remember the horrifying screams of their mother, as her drunken husband approaches her. She will be beaten; it is part of the vicious cycle.

Not only does a victim have trouble identifying with a positive image of a father or mother, but choosing a healthy mate can be extremely difficult. If one views love as taught in the home of origin as screaming, hitting, and verbal degradation, the cycle of abuse will continue. That is why it is often necessary for God to teach those who have been taught incorrectly concerning love. In Isaiah we are told; **"For thy Maker is thine husband; the Lord of hosts is his name..."** Later in this chapter God establishes a covenant of peace, and a promise of kindness, to those who marry him. **(Isaiah 54:5-10)**

Because of the inherent desire a victim possesses to repeat history, he or she must be submissive to God's voice. An abuser does not look like an abuser. Remember Satan disguises himself as an **"angel of light."** **(2 Cor.11:14)** That's why God spoke so clearly to me that I was not to date. He knew I would unintentionally connect with someone Satan had sent to destroy me.

God often needs to keep those who have been in abusive relationships separated to Himself for a time, in order to teach them how He views love. The 13th Chapter of First Corinthians should be a continual study for those trying to break free of addictive relationship. In this chapter Paul defines love as **"patient, love is kind. It does not envy, it does not boast, it is not proud. It is not rude, it is not self-seeking, it is not easily angered, it keeps no record of wrongs. Love does not delight in evil but rejoices with the truth. It always protects, always trusts, always hopes, always perseveres."** **(1 Cor. 13:4-7 NIV)**

Several years ago, a woman I did not know well was committed to the psychiatric ward. A mutual friend felt it was God's will that I go to visit her, so that my victory over depression might testify to her. When I got there, I was horrified by what I saw. The poor woman was the classic example of what I'd seen many times when people "break down." She was bloated from medication and very confused. She had a hideous rash, and tried unsuccessfully to keep from crying.

"Victim" was written all over her. Why had I not seen it before? The last time I saw her we were at a Women's Aglow meeting and she looked like a picture of sophistication in her red suit and well-coiffed hair. Her wedding ring and polished nails reminded me of the handsome "Christian" husband who waited for her at home. So, why was she lying in a bed on the psychiatric ward mumbling gibberish and blinking back tears?

In her desperation to trust someone, her story began to tumble out. Perhaps because she didn't know me, or maybe because she knew I understood by the spirit, she told me her husband abused her. I was shocked. I was more shocked when she said, "Sometimes, he can't even wait until we get out of the parking lot at the church. He'll just lean over and hit me in the mouth, and tell me to shut up." She mumbled something about another woman. Although she had an excellent job, she didn't know where her money went. She said her husband took her checks and told her the money was always gone.

I knew this woman was close to being destroyed, so I said, "God does not want you to live like this." There is a point of a victim's life when they truly can no longer tolerate being a victim. Unfortunately, feeling helpless to change their circumstance, they often try to end their lives.

Too often, we offer these people no hope through the Word. They are being destroyed by Satan, and we use the Word as a gun to kill them. We tell them divorce is a sin, and they are bound to live in hell for the rest of their time on earth. Then we pull Scriptures out of context to convince them that God's love will quit operating in their lives, unless they remain married.

Dave Roberson is a teaching evangelist from Tulsa. His teaching has helped me to study the Bible as God intended. In his tape series, "Meditation-Imagery-Delivery,"*3 Brother Roberson explains how we can never pull verses out of context to accurately interpret God's Word. He says we must always examine the preceding verses and the succeeding verses when studying Scripture.

Because of this teaching I began to study the word "infidel" in a new light. In **1 Timothy 5:8**, Paul tells us that, **"if any provide not for his own, and specially for those of his own house he hath denied the faith, and is worse than an infidel."**

Paul was not talking about a man laid off, or one injured and unable to work. Rather, he was talking about someone who consciously chooses to ignore the needs of his family. Paul nestles this Scripture among several where he commands the widows are to be taken care of by children, family, or the church. Abused wives have become spiritual and in many cases natural widows and we as the church have a responsibility to care for them. Too often they are told they have made their bed, now they must sleep in it.

In 2 Corinthians 6:14-18, Paul tells us we are to have no fellowship with infidels and that we are to be separate, and not touch the unclean thing. Then he says, God will be a Father to us. As Fathers do, he will truly meet our needs.

Let me state quite clearly that I do not advocate divorce. God hates divorce. But God hates even more his people being destroyed, and perishing for lack of knowledge. When people come for help, we must use wisdom. We can no longer tell the mother whose daughter is being sexually abused by her father to go home and pray that God will change the situation. We must be willing to support people in their spirit-led decisions. Most often we need simply to love them and not judge them.

These are the end times, and every kind of imaginable problem will flood the church. As God calls those from the North, South, East, and West to repentance, they will bring in the dysfunctions of the past. There will be sexual abuse, divorce, abortion, and homosexuality. You name it, we will deal with it. These people will come to Christ with their sins, and He will forgive them. But it is our job to teach them how to go and sin no more.

For years, it was very difficult for me to believe that God could use me, because of the sin and sickness of my past. We tell people they are forgiven, and that they are a new creation, then we limit what God will do in their lives.

Once I wrote to Pastor Carlton Pearson. At the time I knew God had called me to a work, but I felt hopeless to do it. God truly chooses the foolish things to confound the wise, calling a little divorced woman who had spent years in and out of psychiatric hospitals. One day, a letter arrived from Brother Pearson. That letter dramatically changed my vision. It said:

"Be encouraged in knowing that we serve a God of second chances. One who loves and forgives and forgets our past trans-

**gressions. God desires to show Himself strong on your behalf.
(2 Chronicles 16:9) God can use the former circumstances in
your life to manifest His power and glory as He daily trans-
forms you more and more into His image and likeness.**

**You have said it right. The truth has made you free. You
can now walk victoriously in light of knowing that.**

**Do not settle for second best in any area of your life. In-
stead seek to avail yourself to all that God wants to do for you.
As you do, you will begin to walk in a new level and dimension
of His blessing."*4**

Pastor Pearson spoke directly to two areas of my life, and I
believe the lives of all those who have been victims. First, God is
a God of second chances. He is able to take circumstances that
Satan created to destroy us, and use them to glorify Himself. We
must believe, as Jeremiah said, that God has promised us **a future
and hope**. (**Jeremiah 29:11 NIV**) We must not limit what God
will do to or through us because of our past hurts or mistakes.

Second, Brother Carlton said not to settle for second best in
any area of life. As a victim, I had unknowingly always felt tar-
nished and second best. I had never stepped out in faith to pursue
God's best, as I did not understand that I was allowed to have His
best. Those of you who have always settled, too, begin to believe
that God wants to do a new thing in your life today.

CHAPTER 8

THE NECESSITY OF HOLINESS

**"Blessed are the pure in heart,
for they shall see God." Matt. 5:8**

Another consequence of sexual abuse is the inability victims possess to stay holy before God, or sometimes faithful to their earthly mates. The guilt of the sin of sexual abuse is not to be placed upon the victim. But, the effects of sexual abuse often cause victims to live a lifestyle of sin and sexual addiction.

In **1 Corinthians 6:18** we are warned to **"flee sexual immorality."** Paul continues in the Scripture to explain that **"he who sins sexually sins against his own body." NIV**

The Full-Life Study Bible text tells us that "sexual immorality is particularly abhorrent to God. More than any other sinful act, it desecrates the body, which is the temple of the spirit. Paul gives us the admonition to flee sexual immorality. The use of the present tense here indicates that the Christian must repeatedly flee sexual immorality."*1

This text defines sexual immorality and impurity to "include not only forbidden intercourse or consummated acts, but also involve any act of sexual gratification with another person other than one's marriage partner achieved by uncovering or exploring the nakedness of that person. The contemporary teaching that sexual intimacy among committed unmarried youth is acceptable as long as it stops short of full sexual union is contrary to the holiness of God..."*2

The seventh commandment found in **Exodus 20:14** forbids

87

adultery. As revealed in the preceding chapter, the unmarried are to become married to the Lord. Therefore, the married and unmarried are commanded to stay faithful to God or to their earthly mate.

God did not tell us over and over in Scripture to deny sexual sin to rob us of physical pleasure. Rather, He wanted us to be aware that sin always produces death in our lives, and later eternal damnation.

Recently, I spoke with a new convert in the church. Within moments, I could see Satan's work of destruction in her life. This beautiful young woman exhibited every symptom of sexual abuse: relationship after relationship, suicidal behavior, anxiety attacks, and hospitalization.   As she shared her past with me, she thought I would be shocked at her history. Instead, I sadly shook my head and said, "You were sexually abused as a child."

She said, "I don't know about that, but I have been actively having sex since I was 6 years old." Now I was shocked. This precious woman didn't understand that she had been violated, although she was obviously quite intelligent. Denial and or memory loss are not uncommon for victims of abuse. My own childhood memories are very sketchy.

I tried to remain calm as I said to her, "6-year-old children do not actively have sex." I asked her if she knew a 6-year-old, and said picture her in your mind. Then I asked her if that child was capable of understanding sex. I told her she had been abused, which had led to a lifestyle of sexual addiction.

In **1 Corinthians 6:19-20**, Paul tells us that our bodies are not our own, we are bought with a price. When I told this girl that she could not continue to have unhealthy relationships, she looked terrified. She cried out, "But how can I be alone?"

God can heal this young woman, but she will have to be willing. Her abuse has affected the majority of her life. It will take time and great effort to be free.

For some abuse victims, addiction to sexual relationship is like an alcoholic's drink, or an addict's drug. This woman will need constant Christian support to break free from her addiction. It will take much more than commanding the unclean spirit out. It will require teaching her about Christ and His ever-present love, helping her to understand that her body is not a bargaining tool to stay aloneness, and showing her steps to avoid temptation.

The church I attend is composed predominantly of people, like this young woman, who must recover from the effects of dysfunction. Literally, hundreds of people who attend Only Believe Ministries Christian Center have valiantly fought to overcome all kinds of addictions to become new creatures in Christ. Because of the varied backgrounds people bring into the church, they must be taught explicitly what God's Word says concerning sin.

Guidelines to Living Sin Free

Several years ago, Pastors, Peter and Phyllis Doseck, detected sexual sin in the lives of some of the singles in the church. Pastor addressed the singles fellowship with guidelines to observe in order to overcome the struggle to stay holy before God. He warned specifically about how the body works. He said, "The body is like a computer. A simple kiss is the switch that sets that computer off." Pastor was not referring to a platonic kiss, but a sexual kiss.

Some in the group might have felt his counsel simplistic, but it is a necessary element to holiness, especially for those who have been sexually abused. Often, victims have allowed their bodies to be the test for what is right or wrong. This test will fail. Earlier, we looked at the fact that victims assume guilt as their bodies often respond pleasurably during violation.

My generation coined a phrase responsible for much moral erosion, "If it feels good, do it." The body is a tactile computer. Physical contact with another will frequently feel good. That does not make it right or holy in God's eyes. After all, we are told in **Hebrews 11:25** that sin is pleasurable for a season. Sin will feel good. Yet the consequences of that sin is always death, according to **Romans 6:23**.

It is not God who zaps us with punishment for our sin. The sin itself activates the curse of the Law resulting in punishment. Often, we feel our sin does not have a consequence, because there is a time period between the sin and the judgment executed. We find an explanation for this in **Ecclesiastes 8:11, "Because sentence against an evil work is not executed speedily, therefore**

the heart of the sons of men is fully set in them to do evil." The curse of the Law is outlined in **Dueteronomy 28:14-68**. The blessing for keeping the Law is contained in the first fourteen verses of the same chapter.

Fornication can become habitual sin. Our conscience becomes hardened to the fact that it is wrong, because our body says it's right. Like other habits that must be broken, an addict must change things that act as stimulus in activating sexual desire. Any physical contact can stimulate victims who have become addictive. It is is important for singles to fellowship in groups, to avoid kissing and prolonged hugs.

Dating is a very serious relationship that we often engage in without prayer or God's permission. When we date, we are entertaining a potential mate. What we think of as a quick dinner could actually end in lifelong commitment. That's why we have to be so careful who we date, or who we kiss. Remember, you'll set off the computer.

Another stimulus in activating sexual desire is masturbation. Satan has deceived the masses that masturbation will satisfy sexual desire. There is always partial truth in Satan's lies. Masturbation will temporarily satisfy sexual desire, but it will ultimately increase the body's appetite.

A good analogy is a smoker's need for a cigarette to satisfy his nicotine craving. Unfortunately, he will desire another cigarette within a few hours to satisfy the next craving.

Instead of masturbation decreasing the sexual appetite, it will actually result in a greater vunerability to sin. Masturbation is uncleanness before the Lord. The word uncleanness is used 11 times in the King James version of the New Testament.*3 Ten times in New Testament Scripture, uncleanness is derived from the Greek word *akatharsia*, meaning impurity, filthiness, or physical or moral uncleanness.*4

In **Galatians 5:19** Paul lists uncleanness among the works of the flesh. He further warns **"that they which do such things shall not inherit the kingdom of God.**" Some Christians might argue that masturbation is not uncleanness. A young Christian woman asked that I help her with sin in her life. She said, "I'm having sex with myself." Her conscience had warned her that masturbation was sin. Yet there must first be a stimulus that results in masturbation.

Once I attended a counseling session with my pastor and a woman with marital problems. Her spouse did not desire to have sex with her, but preferred masturbation. Pastor observed that there was a stimulus causing the woman's husband to masturbate. The most obvious stimulus would be pornography, but "unclean" or lustful thoughts also could create sexual desire.

Satan will try to snare us by bombarding us with impure thoughts. Such thoughts are a form of temptation, not sin. The Sin begins when we begin to activate the thought instead of commanding it leave in Jesus' name. Paul tells us in **2 Corinthians 10:5 "to take captive every thought to make it obedient to Christ."** **NIV**

Satan will also bring thoughts of yesterday to produce a state of sin-consciousness. Many victims literally live in the past replaying scene after scene of unholy acts. Most abuse victims spend much of their lives feeling dirty, guilty, and hopeless.

Thank God for Christ's redeeming blood. The blood that redeemed us on Calvary continues to deliver us daily. We can walk in total freedom and cleansing, but the price we must pay is a lifestyle of holiness. In **Romans 12:1** Paul commands us to present our bodies as a **"living sacrifice unto God."** In the next Scripture he tells us to **"not be conformed to this world, but to be transformed by the renewing of the mind." Romans 12:2** How do we renew our mind? We renew our mind through the Word. Our minds cannot be renewed clouded by drugs and alcohol that loose inhibition and destroy our ability to make righteous decisions.

In **Proverbs 31:4-5** we are told **"It is not for kings to drink wine; nor for rulers to crave beer, lest they drink and forget what the law decrees." (NIV)** The Hebrew literally says: "let there be no drinking." This passage makes no allowance for moderate drinking. The reason kings and rulers are not to drink intoxicating drink is that they might otherwise forget the law. Such drinking would weaken them morally and lead them to disobey God's law and pervert justice.

Victims of abuse must maintain an unbending resolve concerning alcohol and drugs. Often depressants are used as a type of self-medication to control or dull the pain the victim's lifestyle creates. Tranquilizers given to alleviate symptoms of depression can be abused, too, if not taken as prescribed.

In many denominations drinking is not viewed as sin. Christians often ask, "A glass of wine won't send me to Hell, right?"

But for an addictive person, a glass of wine is a dangerous snare. There will be another glass, then another, followed by language and behavior that deviate from the Highway of Holiness God has commanded us to walk. Alcohol and drugs give Satan a direct medium to work through. He already has robbed so many of us of peaceful yesterdays. Why allow him a door into our tomorrows? Even if you do not have an addictive personality, it is dangerous for a victim to use any mood-altering substance.

Through this book we are studying specific ways to cope with the emotions that result from abuse. We are also learning to live life victim-free. But it will take a conscious, consistent effort to walk in all Christ purchased for us at Calvary. In order to have the victorious mind of Christ, and not the mind of a defeated victim, we must observe the pathway of purity of our Savior. We must lay our unhealthy addictions at the feet of Jesus, and become addicted to God's Word and His work.

As we seek to follow God's path, Satan will come to tempt us. But remember, **"God is faithful; He will not let you be tempted beyond what you can bear. But when you are tempted He will also provide a way out." 1 Corinthians 10:13** Pray, believing God will show you the way out of temptation. He is always faithful.

It is never too late. It doesn't matter what happened to us as children, or how we reacted later. What matters is what we do for Christ today.

If you or one you are counseling has lived a lifestyle of sexual sin following the initial violation, I have great news for you. Christ's blood is enough to pay the price. But first, you must ask Him to be the Lord and Savior of your life. Then you must ask Him to forgive your sins, promising Him you will go and sin no more.

In **Hebrews 10:17**, we see that God not only forgives our sins, He forgets them. **"Their sins and lawless acts I will remember**

no more." (**NIV**) We, too, must forget the wrongs we have done in our ignorance. We can be holy only if we begin to see ourselves holy through Him. Truly, "**if anyone is in Christ, he is a new creation; old things have passed away; behold, all things have become new.**" **2 Corinthians 5:17 NKJ**

If you have never accepted Jesus Christ as the Lord and Savior of your life, or if you have not been walking the Highway of Holiness which God requires, please say the following prayer out loud:

Father God,

I have been hurt and abused, and I have hurt and abused myself and others. I need your precious Son, Jesus Christ, to come into my heart and be the Lord and Savior of my life. Lord Jesus, I invite you to live in my heart today. I ask you to forgive me for the sins of my past.

Lord, teach me how to live pure and holy before you. Send your grace to deliver me from the power of sin. Lead me in the paths of righteousness for your name's sake. I make a decision to serve you from this day in Jesus' name.

CHAPTER NINE

TRUST

I vowed to never trust a man,
Or woman with my pain.
After finding the Creator's hand
Human help seemed ever vain.

Then as I wept in bitterness
Broken-hearted on my knees
The answer came while praying
You must trust one of these.

For though men are not perfect
Nor women always wise
They are my Spirit's mouthpiece
Between the earth and Heaven's skies.

Dedicated to Ginni, who taught me
to trust Jesus.

Christina

One of the most devastating long-term effects of sexual abuse at a young age is the destruction of the ability to trust. When the abuse is perpetrated by a supposedly loving parent or other close relative, the child's inner core is ravaged. There seems to be an almost innate desire in the human soul to trust others. With abuse, there comes a knowing that this is not to be.

I have heard Christians counsel others that they must trust people. Yet, God tell us in **Psalm 118:9, "It is better to trust in the Lord than to put confidence in man**."

We continue to point people to other people when we need first to point them to Almighty God. David had a revelation that man would fail. He himself had failed when confronted with his carnal desire for Bathsheba. David also realized that our Heavenly Father never fails us. It is not that people mean to fail us. It is merely that they are human, and as such are lacking.

In order to begin to trust God we must begin to identify Him as a being far too awesome for our human comprehension. We must begin to realize that He is not a man, but that He is divine. **"God is not a man, that He should lie; neither the son of man, that He should repent: hath He said, and shall He not do it?.." Numbers 23:19**

For many victims the term father carries a frighteningly negative connotation. They must reach past their earthly experience and toward a heavenly Father, who is in no way a man, but in every way interested only in their good.

Once I attended a Christian concert, where I learned that I was distrustful of God's motivation in my life. During the concert, performer Craig Smith talked about people who, because of dysfunctional upbringings, were not able to wholly trust God. He spelled the word, "wholly," and it literally flashed in my mind like a neon sign.

During the long drive home, the Lord spoke inside my inner being, and told me I was one of the people who did not wholly trust Him. Although I have never heard God's voice in an audible way, He often speaks in that still small voice from within.

I began to argue with Him, thinking it was probably my own mind, or Satan taunting me. Arguing with God is futile. He is always right. He spoke one more time, and asked me why, if I wholly trusted Him, I had Plan A for when God works, and Plan B for when He fails.

Immediately, I knew that was the truth. I always had a backup plan for when those I cared for let me down. It was no different with God. I repented and began to weep. I told Him I was so sorry that I did not wholly trust Him. I realized I did not know how to trust completely and I asked Him for help.

I had to journey back into my past to understand where the root of mistrust had grown. Because of my earthly father's weaknesses, he was incapable of keeping his word.

When I was a small child Dad usually drank heavily on Saturday night. He would get drunk, feel lightheaded and energetic, and promise to take us to the zoo or on a picnic the next day. I could barely sleep waiting for the promised outing. Then the next morning, in the midst of an alcoholic hangover, he would either say he never promised, or that he'd take us another time.

At first, I remember feeling angry and betrayed when this happened. I would plead and beg, "This isn't fair, you promised." Then, after a period of years, a bitterness arose in my heart and I began to disbelieve not only everything my dad said, but what others in my life said, too.

At a young age I realized that people often failed to keep their promises. I viewed God as a man incapable of keeping His promises, too. After all I had been told that God would protect me from harm. After I began to be sexually abused I blamed not only God, but myself. Somehow I should have prevented my abuser's sexual feelings for me. I should have acted differently, dressed differently.

Then one Sunday as I sat in church, a 10-year-old girl approached the altar for prayer. She looked so innocent in her little cotton dress, marching forward unaware of her undeveloped body, aware only that she was going to God's altar to get what she needed. I smiled at her, as she boldly approached the throne of her Father, confident that she would be blessed. It was then the Holy Spirit spoke.

"Could she help herself?"

"What do you mean?" I asked.

"Could she help herself?" He repeated.

That little child was so fragile, so dependent on those who cared for her. I had judged myself as an adult woman with the knowledge and wisdom that an adult possesses. I had assumed guilt for a crime I'd never committed. Worse, I had been serving a life sentence with no hope of reprieve.

Once I went for counseling I shared with the Christian counselor that I had been sexually abused as a child. I went only once to that counselor, however, as upon this statement she looked directly at my body and a look of curiosity crossed her face.

I caution you that if you react to a victim's sharing in this manner, she will instantly distrust you and stop sharing. Those body parts were probably not there at the time of the violation, anyway, as they were not developed yet. In most cases, a small child was violated, not a grown woman.

In order for that small child to survive, the ability to trust is literally discarded. It becomes a given for abuse victims that they will be violated, or that they will be disappointed by the lack of integrity in others. They begin to mistrust everyone, including themselves.

I lived my life concerned about what others thought of me. Victims have an inner knowing about concealing things from outsiders. Everyone is an outsider except those who live in the circle of dysfunction. In order to have people like me, I forfeited the right to have opinions or needs. I was like a person who did not exist. A sort of human chameleon who would be whatever others expected me to be. This way seemed to be the path of least resistance. I continually thought:

"If I'm nice to others, they will be nice to me. Everyone will like me, and no one will hurt me again."

This is often the victim's role. We will be hurt time and time again as we surround ourselves with people who are destructive.

My clone-like personality caused me to become successful as a corporate sales representative upon my completion of college. I learned how to manipulate people at an early age in order to survive, and my ability to manipulate went into full motion as a sales person. I lost any connection with who I was and became who I thought others desired me to be.

I had been programmed to believe that success is measured by the kind of car you drive, the home you live in, and the money in your bank account. I did not know there is a success that can only be measured by the peace in your heart.

I worked at a feverish pace to get promoted into management with my corporation. After four years, I met with one of the big bosses to discuss my move up. I had been a single mother when they hired me. I had neglected my son to travel and climb the corporate ladder. Building a better life for him had been my dream.

A well-paid executive from top management took me to lunch and told me the company was pleased with my work and ready to promote me. He said quite matter of factly, "There is a small problem. You'll have to do something about your son."

I pretended not to understand the impact of that sentence, and asked him to excuse me as I needed to use the restroom. I remember vividly holding onto the sink basin, and looking at my reflection in the mirror. I thought, all these years of working late, staying in hotels, being away from my son, and now, this? Once again, in one moment's time the dream of the last five years was destroyed.

When the rage subsided, I returned to the table and resumed our conversation. I said, "I think perhaps you've misunderstood my motivation. I've been working to provide a good life for my son. The only thing I'm going to do about him is to take good care of him, as he is my priority."

Even though I was not yet a Christian, I thank God that His spirit had been wooing me, and I had realized what a great gift from God my little boy had been.

This event coupled with a destructive relationship with an emotionally abusive man led me back to the psychiatric ward where I had been a patient 10 years earlier. Although I was 32 chronologically, a very hurt child surfaced, one whose wounds had been reopened. I was in great pain. My dreams were once more destroyed by the deception of those close to me.

But this time was different. I ran to God instead of away from

Him. I had nowhere else to go. I was wounded and bleeding, and without hope. God began to show me His path as He had shown Moses and the children of Israel in the midst of their wilderness. It was there the cloud that led me out first appeared. (**Exodus 13:21**) At night, the pillar of fire showed me I was not alone and there was a path that I must take.

It was not easy to learn to trust God. First I had to learn to die to self. **"For we know that our old self was crucified with Him so that the body of sin might be rendered powerless, that we should no longer be slaves to sin—because anyone who has died has been freed from sin. Now if we died with Christ, we believe that we will also live with Him."** (**Romans 6:6-8 NIV**)

I had to learn to die to the rebellious nature that I had used to survive. I had to die to the sin that had become a way of life for me. I could use no more excuses to deny that I must serve God as He commanded.

I began to see that as I walked the path God ordained, His hand was ever present to lead, protect and comfort me. For the first year and a half of my Christian walk, I floundered from church to church. I had to be taught the truth in order to live it. Churches weak in the Word will never set a victim free. As I began to hunger for God, He led me by His Spirit.

In 1988, God led me to a growing church in a small community in rural Ohio. My pastors, Peter and Phyllis Doseck, became the lifeline God used to help me develop relationship with others. I knew God had supernaturally planted me in Only Believe Ministries Christian Center. At times, I rebelled and wanted to leave. Sometimes people offended me. Sometimes my pastors did not understand my needs. But God understood my needs.

I have learned to trust God because I have been taught to understand that God's Word is infallible. He is not a man, and His integrity is divine, not human. Through the Holy Spirit, I have realized that my pastors are human beings who make mistakes. Yet I have come to know them as people who desire to serve God with their whole hearts, and to lead others to the knowledge that Jesus Christ is the only perfect one. My pastors do not have all the answers, but they have taught me to know the One who does.

In **Hebrews 10:25** we are told, "**not forsaking the assembling together, as the manner of some is; but exhorting one another; and so much the more, as ye see the day approaching.**" God knew how evil the world would become in the end times. He knew there would be hurt people crying out for help. This is why we are told to meet together with our brothers and sisters in Christ. God wants us to encourage one another to continue in the faith.

Learning to trust God is possible only through getting to know Him through Scripture. "**But let him who glories glory in this, that he understands and knows Me.**" (Jeremiah 9:24 NKJ)

We are to glory in knowing God who does good on our behalf. A good God is not one who causes bad things to happen in our lives. God does not give us car wrecks and cancer. We have attributed things to God that He would never do. He loves us and desires to see good on our behalf. In **James 1:17** we see that "**Every good gift and every perfect gift is from above, and cometh down from the Father of lights, with whom there is no variableness, neither shadow of turning.**"

God is not double-minded. It is never His desire that His children be victims of abuse. **3 John 2** says, "**Beloved, I wish above all things that thou mayest prosper and be in health, even as thy soul prospers.**"

God desires to help us, and to heal us. We must understand that He is the author of the good, not the creator of the bad in our lives. He will make a good come out of each bad we encounter, but it is not His desire that we encounter the bad. We live in a fallen world and Satan is the god of this world. Satan is our enemy, not our beloved father.

Many of us were taught that God wants us to suffer so He can teach us something. We must be retaught that God does not want us to suffer, but that He will use whatever our circumstances are to help us be more dependent on Him.

The only way we can learn about the good things that God wants to do in our lives is through the local church. In **John 10:10** Jesus said, "**...I am come that they might have life, and that they might have it more abundantly.**" He does not want us to have a limited life, but a life of victory and freedom in His Spirit. We must be taught what His promises are through the truth of His Word.

"And ye shall know the truth, and the truth shall make you free." (John 8:32) The only way to know the truth is to hear the truth. Once we hear it, we must continue to keep the Word activated in our hearts. We cannot merely hear the Word once, we must live in Scripture. **"If ye continue in my word, then are ye my disciples indeed; and ye shall know the truth..."** (John 8:31-32)

We must continue day by day for our entire lifetime to get to know our Heavenly Father. We must aggressively fight those thoughts of doubt about His intention of good in our lives. We need to become a part of a local church that is not afraid to teach the totality of God's truth. If you don't see deliverance and changed lives in your church, something is wrong. Seek God and ask Him where you need to be to get the help you need to be set free.

When I first attended Only Believe Ministries, I was unable to speak about things that deeply concerned me. I could not talk in person, but I could write letters. I called this series of letters the "Pastor, my Pastor" letters. I would pour out my heart in these letters and explain things I was unable to say in person. I wrote these letters for more than two years. Most of the letters did not require a reply, as they were a kind of theraputic tool. But once in awhile, my pastor would give me a bit of counsel, or my pastor's wife would just give me a hug and tell me she loved me. This relationship helped me begin to trust.

Some people coming from abusive backgrounds will go back to those who have repeatedly hurt them for counsel. Maybe you have not been hurt physically, but time after time, you go to an emotionally unavailable person with life's questions. Or you go to people who are so controlled by their own fears that they will speak their fear upon you.

In a dysfunctional family, we run back to people we know offer us no assistance in trouble. This reinforces the feeling that we are not worthwhile and that our problems, goals, and visions are of no significance. This is incorrect thinking. But we begin to see ourselves as others see us.

The best analogy for this type of non-productive behavior is the horse that repeatedly returns to the dry well. Like that horse, we return to the same watering hole where we know there is no water. We must break this pattern of behavior in Jesus' name. After all, these people do not mean to withhold water from us; they simply don't have it to give.

"If any man thirst, let him come unto me, and drink," Jesus said. **"He that believeth on me, as the Scripture hath said, out of his belly shall flow rivers of living water." (John 7:37-38)**

The living water which is the Holy Spirit is our spirit of counsel, direction, and comfort. Believers should never go to unbelievers with their hurts of yesterday, or their visions of tomorrow. In **2 Corinthians 6:14**, Paul warns, **"Be not unequally yoked together with unbelievers; for what fellowship has righteousness with unrighteousness?"**

In order to heal the pain of the past and gain insight into the visions of our tomorrows, we must first seek the Holy Spirit. We must ask Him to lead us to a local church with a pastor who will counsel us according to the anointed Word of the Lord. Then if we need help in specific areas, we must ask the Spirit to lead us to a trusted confidant who can minister to us in those areas.

Recently, a new convert entered our church. As a pastor does not have time to disciple each new individual in a large church, they are assigned a mature believer who will walk the beginnings of their Christian walk with them. This new believer was a single young woman with a lifelong history of sexual, physical, and verbal abuse.

Since the young woman's background was not disclosed, she was placed with a married woman who was a strong believer. During a phone conversation, these women agreed that because of their different backgrounds they did not feel it was God's will for them to be together. The new convert asked if I would work with her, as I was single at the time, and a former victim, too.

This girl showed amazing wisdom in requesting someone who had once been like her. For months, we met a few hours each week. I shared many of the things with her that are in this book.

She also shared with me. We must always remain teachable to be effective in ministering to others.

She taught me it is vital to find a trusted confidant you can share with, one who will understand. I'm not saying everyone who works with the abused must be a former victim. But it gives victims hope when they see "one of their kind" achieving good things in the real world. This is what **Victory over Suffering** is all about, becoming victorious despite circumstances that Satan used to try to destroy you.

There is one more area of the trust issue that must be addressed. That is the spirit of control, or actually overcontrol. Many of us who were victims become controllers in an effort to ensure that we will not be victimized again. This will not keep us safe from violation, and it will make those around us miserable.

Control is the inability to trust that God can carry out His plan, so we "help" God by manipulating people and circumstances in our lives. Often we have been controlled for so long that it is just natural for us to react as we have been taught.

When we begin to operate under this spirit of control, we soon find ourselves exhausted and unable to carry the burdens in our lives. Yet Jesus said, **"Come to me, all you who are weary and burdened, and I will give you rest. Take my yoke upon you and learn from me, for I am gentle and humble in heart, and you will find rest for your souls. For my yoke is easy and my burden is light." (Matthew 11:28-30 NIV)**

Jesus said His burden is light, because He does not expect us to carry our troubles upon our own shoulders. Rather, Peter tells us to **"Cast all your care upon Him; for He cares for you." (1 Peter 5:7 NIV)** Because all those we have trusted have let us down, we don't trust God enough to let Him handle our problems. But if we truly want to be the disciples God intends us to be, we must let go of control. The Holy Spirit cannot operate in our lives unless there is a liberty in our spirit man.

We control others thinking we know what's best, hoping the love in the relationship will deepen. Instead those we control begin to rebel. They resent us for binding them to us.

For years, I was frantic that someone would try to abuse my son. I would tell him over and over, "Don't let anyone touch you in private places. Tell me if someone threatens you. Watch out for everyone."

One day at age 10, he looked at me with frustation and yelled, "I'm not you." My son does not raise his voice often. I was startled as I heard the anger and truth that he spat at me so vehemently. All his life I had treated him as if he were me and that my circumstances were his.

If you see yourself in either the inability to trust or the tendency to control, please don't feel alone. Most of us who have been victims and who are honest will admit that trust and control are ongoing problem areas.

The good news is that Jesus Christ came to set us free in every area of life. Once you begin to heal in the area of trust, it will be easier to relinquish control of your life to God. Trust, like forgiveness, takes time to achieve. It requires getting to know God for who He truly is. As you begin to trust Him, you will see His plan is far better for you and those you love than any plan you could outline with the carnal mind.

If you have seen yourself in this chapter, please say this prayer out loud with me:

Dear God,

I don't know how to trust. I'm sorry that I've lived my life without wholly casting all my cares upon you. I'm tired, Father, of carrying my own burdens, and the burdens of those I love. Please teach me to let go of the problems and hurts that I cling to. Lord, I'm like a small child who has a poisonous pill cupped tightly in my little fist, refusing to let go, as it is mine. God, I don't want it anymore. I extend my open hand to you. Here are my hurts, my pain, my cares. I give them to you, God. Teach me who you are and help me to become more like you with each passing day, in Jesus' name.

CHAPTER TEN

SOMETHING TO LOOK FORWARD TO

**"Be ye also patient; stablish your hearts: for
the coming of the Lord draweth nigh." James 5:8**

Victory over Suffering has been a labor of love. As victims
we share a kinship of the soul. It is my only desire that in some
way, this book has given you hope to continue in your quest for
total healing. I pray your life will be different knowing it is possible to survive against all odds.

Just a few short years ago, when God had set me free in so
many areas, I found myself lacking. I lacked a purpose, a goal,
and a sense of direction. Although I was functioning well from
day to day — remember this was a miracle for someone who was
supposed to die in a mental institution — I had nothing to look
forward to.

Then through prayer, I found my purpose: I desired to help
others. It was at this time that the revelation came that **"God hath
chosen the foolish things of the world to confound the wise;
and God hath chosen the weak things of the world to confound
the things which are mighty; and base things of the world and
things which are despised, hath God chosen, yea, and things
which are not, to bring to nought things that are: That no flesh
should glory in His presence." (1 Corinthians 1:27-29)**

I gained this revelation through Kathryn Kuhlman's ministry
tapes. Even though Ms. Kuhlman died in 1976, her tapes and books
live on. Kathryn spoke how God's calling came to those who
knew they were unable to achieve without dependence on Him.
She frequently quoted a verse from **Isaiah 42:8 "I am the Lord:**

that is my name: and my glory will I not give to another."

Kathryn Kuhlman knew God would not share His glory with any man or woman. Often, He uses people the world would label as throwaways — empty, broken vessels who know they can do nothing without God orchestrating it.

We are all called to a position of servitude in God's kingdom. There is no greater or lesser calling in Christ. Rather we are one body that functions dependent on one another. For me a desire rose up to see fragmented people like myself set free by God's power. I knew it took me years to learn to walk in the freedom purchased at Calvary, and I began to strive to teach others the way to that freedom.

In the King James version of the Bible, the word "addicted" is used only one time. In **1 Corinthians 16:15**, Paul talks of the house of Stephanas and says, **"they have addicted themselves to the ministry of the saints."** I asked the Lord to take the pain of my past and addict me to ministering to others still in pain.

For years secular psychiatrists had told me to look inward to find answers for myself. When I stopped looking within and started looking to God, I found His answers often came while helping others. Even Jesus **"came not to be ministered unto, but to minister, and to give His life a ransom for many." Mark 10:45**

I know what you're thinking, dear one. You think I don't understand how inadequate and broken you feel. I'm not telling you to go out and tackle the world. I'm just asking you to listen closely to God's voice, as He begins to use you to help others. It may be a small thing like baking cookies for a neighbor, or helping an elderly woman cross the street. Just begin doing the small things that God shows you, and watch how your life will begin to change. As you submerge yourself in the needs of others you will forget your inadequacies in the midst of their needs. Despise not small things: It is through faithfulness in the small things that we become ruler over much.

Many times God will call us to do things we are unable to do in our own ability. For example, God sometimes requires me to preach in front of congregations to share His word. You might not find that unusual unless you know that in the natural, I am terrified of public speaking. But public speaking and preaching are two entirely different arenas. One requires an eloquent command of the English language. The other requires the anointing that only the Holy Spirit possesses.

Perhaps you feel overcome today with a vision that God has given you. You feel inadequate, underqualified, and just plain scared. Good news. My definition of **grace** is **God's ability to do, on our behalf, what we could not do ourselves.**

In order to understand God's grace, let's take a look at Paul's thorn. In the 12th chapter of 2 Corinthians Paul is pleading with God to remove a thorn from his flesh. Erroneous teaching that this thorn was physical sickness has confused Christians into believing that sickness glorifies God. The only time that sickness glorifies God is when our sickness is miraculously touched by the healing power of our Master's hand.

"To keep me from becoming conceited because of these surpassingly great revelations, there was given me a thorn in my flesh, a messenger of Satan, to torment me. Three times I pleaded with the Lord to take it away from me. But he said to me, My grace is sufficient for you, for my power is made perfect in weakness. Therefore I will boast all the more gladly about my weaknesses, so that Christ's power may rest on me. That is why, for Christ's sake, I delight in weaknesses, in insults, in hardships, in persecutions, in difficulties. For when I am weak, then I am strong." 2 Corinthians 12:7-10 NIV

Paul pleaded with God to remove his thorn. God's answer tells Paul that His grace is enough to overcome any weakness. God is not double-minded. He did not say His power is made perfect in sickness. Rather, He said His power is made perfect in weakness. I am too weak to speak to large groups in the natural man. But through the spiritual man, **"I can do all things through Christ who strengthens me." Philippians 4:13 NKJ**

The prophet Joel also had a revelation that God's grace would be sufficient to see us through every God-ordained vision. He said, **"Let the weak say, I am strong." Joel 3:10**

The weak are strong not by the might of their arm, or the power of their hand, but through God's Holy Spirit. Joel spoke of the outpouring of grace that would come upon God's people beckoning in the last and greatest revival. God's Holy Spirit is the Spirit of Grace that will be poured upon us as the day of the Lord approaches. **"And afterward, I will pour out my Spirit on all people."** **Joel 2:28 NIV**

Joel said, **"Afterward, I will pour out my Spirit on all people."** Did you ever ask yourself, after what? Again, let's refer to Dave Roberson's method of studying Scripture in context. In order to understand verse 2:28, let's jump back up to verse 2:25. Joel records the Lord as saying,

"I will restore to you the years that the locust has eaten,... You shall eat in plenty and be satisfied, and praise the name of the Lord your God, who has dealt wondrously with you: and my people shall never be put to shame." **Joel 2:25-26 NKJ**

After what will God pour His Spirit on us? After He restores the years the enemy has taken from our lives. Satan is a thief who comes to rob us, but God is a God of restoration. Through Jesus we have a legal right to regain all the lost possessions Satan has stolen.

I have a teen-age son named Zachary whom I love more than life itself. But my heart ached for a daughter's love, too. When I was 35, God gave me a precious 17-year-old girl to spiritually mother. Her name is Stacey. I could not love her more if she were my own. Stacey filled a desire not only of daughter, but today, she has matured into a committed Christian and wonderful friend.

As Stacey read the first chapter of this book, she became very troubled. She's a very sensitive young woman with mercy as her primary motivational gifting. I said, "What's wrong, Stacey?"

She said, "Christina, it's so sad."

I realized then that I had not shared much of my early life with her, as it had not been relevant to her spiritual upbringing. Reading the black and white facts of my life before Christ, the hospitalizations, the suicide attempts and the abuse saddened my spiritual daughter. Yes, I suppose the first chapter is very depressing. But I pray that this last chapter will be just as encouraging. I am not that troubled child anymore. I am a new creature who is a product of the miracle restoration of God's power.

As I write the final pages of this book, it is once again

Christmas day. I wanted to finish this work by Christmas as my gift to our beloved Savior. The only gift we have to offer Jesus is ourselves. Our hearts, our lives, and our desires are what He really wants. On a daily basis He wants our obedience in following the plan that He lays before us.

For me, this book has been a part of that plan, as was that Christmas spent 14 years ago in the shelter for battered women. In the chapter on forgiveness, I wrote how I felt that Christmas Eve as I looked upon the faces of those women and children who were victims of abuse. I did not know God at that time, but as I cried out to Him, I felt a peace I'd never known.

Today, I live in that peace. It is the peace that comes only through knowing Jesus Christ as Lord and Savior. It is the peace that passes all understanding that keeps your heart and mind in the midst of all adversity. It is the peace that never fails, nor forsakes those who keep their eyes ever focused on Him. I have found that peace through Him and my purpose as I reach out to others, always pointing them back to the Cross of Calvary.

Sometimes I fail in that which I purpose to do, but I take courage in the story of Peter. Jesus told Peter that, before the cock crowed, Simon Peter would deny Him three times. As they led Jesus away for trial and later crucifixion Peter followed at a distance. Jesus had spoken in prophetic truth. When asked whether he was one of Jesus' followers, Peter denied ever knowing Jesus.

But Jesus, knowing this test was to come to Simon Peter, and knowing he would fail the test, had interceded for his disciple. At the Last Supper, Jesus warned Peter of his upcoming denial, and reassured him of his ultimate victory. **"Simon, Simon, Satan has asked to sift you as wheat. But I have prayed for you, Simon, that your faith may not fail. And when you have turned back, strengthen your brothers." Luke 22:31 NIV**

Jesus is praying right now that your faith will not fail. It is not your faith in yourself, but your faith in Him. After Peter denied Jesus, Scripture says he went out and wept bitterly. Perhaps, today you are in a place of remorse for the way your life has been.

I remember spending several Christmases in psychiatric facilities feeling abandoned and hopeless. What I didn't know then was that Jesus himself was praying. (**Luke 22:31**) No matter what has happened to you, or what wrongs you have committed, take comfort in knowing that Jesus is praying for you that your faith will not fail. After you are strengthened by His prayer, make a decision to go forth and help your brothers and sisters who are still suffering.

These are the end times, and the evil will cause millions to suffer. Widespread sexual abuse is a sign of the soon coming of our Lord and Savior Jesus Christ. But many who have been abused have difficulty believing that Jesus is coming back. They doubt the integrity of His Word because they have been lied to and abandoned by those they trusted.

How is sexual abuse a sign of His coming? Let's look at **2 Timothy 3:1-3, "...in the last days perilous times shall come. For men shall be lovers of their own selves, covetous... without natural affection..."**

To be covetous is to be desirous of something that doesn't belong to you. To touch the private parts of an innocent child's body is a sin that will be dealt with harshly. It is the theft of that which belongs solely to God. The Lord guards the innocence of His children.

Jesus warns of the punishment for violating the innocent in **Matthew 18:6 "But whoso shall offend one of these little ones which believe in me, it were better for him that a millstone were hanged about his neck, and that he were drowned in the depth of the sea."**

In the Book of Malachi, God tells us that He will send **"Elijah the prophet before the coming of the great and dreadful day of the Lord: And he shall turn the heart of the fathers to the children, and the heart of the children to their fathers..."**
Malachi 4:5-6

The Holy Spirit is calling us to arms today. As the day of Christ's return approaches, so does the day of His judgment. Those who have been abused must reach out in prayer to those bound by the unclean spirit. Whether they are victims or victimizers, they need to be set free by God's power.

As God's people begin to talk about abuse and acknowledge its rampant existence, we will be able to confront the plan of the enemy head on. We will no longer perish for lack of knowledge, and our children will be warned and protected from the devil's devices.

As the latter rain begins to fall, the glory of the Lord will heal broken hearts and soften hardened ones. Hearts that have been bound by a lifetime of sexual perversion will be changed instantly as a spirit of repentance comes to our land. Truly, God will use our prayers as the weapon to return the hearts of the fathers to the children. God will use the weapon of forgiveness to turn the heart of the children to the fathers.

The only epistle Paul charges us to read to all the brethren is the first book of Thessalonians (**1 Thes. 5:27**). This epistle explains the second coming of Jesus Christ. Paul tells us Jesus will:

"...descend from heaven with a shout, with the voice of the archangel, and with the trump of God and the dead in Christ shall rise first: Then we which are alive and remain shall be caught up together with them in the clouds, to meet the Lord in the air: and so shall we ever be with the Lord. Wherefore comfort one another with these words."
1 Thessalonians 4:16-18

Be comforted in knowing that the greatest thing we have to look forward to is Jesus' coming. He will come to free us from the evil and pain of this Earth. This is the hope of our salvation that we will live forever in the presence of our Savior.

Don't let the devil deceive you and rob you of your hope. Jesus is coming back soon. In His mercy, He wants those who have abused us to know that forgiveness is available at the Cross. He wants those who have been abused to believe He is coming for them. In **Hebrews 9:28**, we are told, **"and unto them that look for Him shall He appear the second time without sin unto salvation."**

The second time Christ appears He will **"not bear sin, but bring salvation to those who are waiting for Him." Hebrews 9:28 NIV** Dear friend, be waiting for His appearing.

Until Jesus comes, the Holy Spirit is searching the Earth for those He can save and heal. He has healed me and enlisted me in His healing army. This is the **Victory over Suffering.**

God has given me a miraculous gift to be "**sitting here, dressed and in my right mind**" this Christmas day. It is no less a miracle for me than it was for the demoniac at the Tomb of the Gadarenes in the fifth chapter of Mark. Jesus cast a legion of demons out of that man. His countrymen were amazed when they saw this crazy man "**sitting and dressed, and in his right mind." Mark 5:15**

The man from the tombs wanted to follow Jesus. But Jesus told him to go home and tell his family and friends the great things the Lord had done for him. God wanted me to tell you the great things He has done for me, too.

Our heavenly Father is no respecter of people. (**Acts 10:34**) What He did for me, He'll do for you. **Hebrews 13:8** says, **"Jesus Christ the same yesterday, today, and forever."** No matter how hopeless your circumstances seem, remember, we serve the God of the impossible. I pray His miracle-working power will touch you and make you whole in Jesus' name.

NOTES

Introduction
1) Jan Frank, A Door of Hope (San Bernardino, CA: Here's Life Publishers, 1987) P. 16
2)Lois Timnick, "22% in Survey were Child Abuse Victims," Los Angeles Times (August 25, 1985)

Chapter Two, "Abused and Abuser"
1) Kathleen Bremner/Candace Walters, My Daughter is a Lesbian," Today's Christian Woman, Jan.-Feb. 1994, pp.36-37
2)Glenna Whitley, "The Seduction of Donnie Porter," Redbook Magazine, April 1993, p.98
3) "   "
4) "   "
5) James Strong, S.t.d., LL.D, The Comprehensive Concordance of the Bible, Iowa Falls, Iowa, World Bible Publishers, Inc., Hebrew and Chaldee Dictionary, p. 115
6) Glenna Whitley, "The Seduction of Donnie Porter," Redbook Magazine, April 1993, p.98

Chapter Three, "Fear"
1) Pastor Peter Doseck, "Fear" tape series, Only Believe Ministries Christian Center, Botkins, Ohio

Chapter Four, "Confidence through Christ"
1) Albert Ellis, Ph.D., "How to Live with and without Anger," (1985) Citadel Press, New York, N.Y. pp.83-90
2)"   "
3) "Twelve Steps and Twelve Traditions," New York, N.Y., Alcoholics Anonymous Publishing World Services, Inc., 1985 p.34

Chapter Five, "Rage"
1) Norvel Hayes, Believer's Convention, August 21, 1981 Tape #21
2) Webster's Dictionary, Springfield, Mass., R.R. Donnelley & Sons Co., 1961, p. 706
3)James Strong, S.t.d., LL.D, The Comprehensive Concordance of the Bible, Iowa Falls, Iowa, World Bible Publishers, Inc., Greek Dictionary, p. 9
4)" " Hebrew and Chaldee Dictionary p.74

Chapter Six, "Forgiveness"
1) James Strong, S.t.d., LL.D, The Comprehensive Concordance of the Bible, Iowa Falls, Iowa, World Bible Publishers, Inc., Greek Dictionary, p.16
2) " ", Hebrew and Chaldee Dictionary, p. 86
3) Pastor Peter Doseck, "Forgiveness" tape series, Only Believe Ministries Christian Center, Botkins, Ohio

Chapter Seven, "Love, Addiction, and Relationships"
1) Rochelle Twining, Founder, former Director, Crossroads Crises Center, Lima, Ohio
2) Crossroads Crises Center, Lima, Ohio, Intake form, May 1981
3) Dave Roberson, "Meditation-Imagery-Delivery" tape series, Dave Roberson Ministries, Tulsa, Ok
4) Pastor Carlton Pearson, Higher Dimensions, Tulsa, Ok.

Chapter Eight, "Necessity of Holiness"
1) Donald C. Stamps, General Editor, The Full Life Study Bible, King James version, Grand Rapids, Mi., Zondervan Publishing House, p. 1778
2) " " - "Standards of Sexual Morality" p. 1964
3)James Strong, S.t.d., LL.D, The Comprehensive Concordance of the Bible, Iowa Falls, Iowa, World Bible Publishers, Inc., p.1089
4) " " Greek Dictionary, p.9

ACKNOWLEDGMENTS

Thank you, Lord, for healing me so that I could reach out to touch the lives of others. Thank you for sending me a patient Editor and encourager in the person of Michael Lackey. Thanks to JoAnne Koch, my consulting Editor for freely sharing her wisdom to create "Victory over Suffering." Thanks to the Holy Spirit for the divine appointment with JoAnne.

Heartfelt gratitude to watercolor artist Marge Brandt for the gift of the book's cover.

Thank you to Kim Hardesty for all the hours spent typing the book's manuscript, and to David Kirchenbauer who allowed us to "indefinitely borrow" his word processor.

Thanks to each of you who have been partners in prayer to birth this book. Special thanks to Brother Stan Jacobs, Debra Tibbs and Ginni Guarnieri for their unceasing prayer support, and to my precious pastors, Peter and Phyllis Doseck, for having hearts like God's heart and for feeding me with knowledge and understanding.

A big God Bless You to Julie Christopher, founder of "Beauty for Ashes" and Access Counseling for Group Leader training, and spiritual support. Thanks and love to Dwight Wisener, who spent his last days on earth encouraging me to go forward with the vision for "New Creation Ministries."

Special thanks to Emerson Joseph for his technical assistance.

Thanks to Tim Wolfrum, and CSS Publishing for making **Victory over Suffering** a reality.

Thank you to all of you, who have suffered the pain of victimization, but have asked God for the courage to walk the path of healing.

To contact Christina Ryan for
speaking engagements please write:

Rev. Christina M. Ryan
New Creation Ministries
P.O. Box 715
Lima, OH 45802-0715